Everything in Life has a Purpose

By Josh Grove

Contributions by: Scott Grove and Lisa Grove-Raider

Editor: Eliza Kalfa

Creative Work: Amy Duncan

Supported by: Dylan Breger

Table of Contents

<u>Prologue</u>

Steve Grove:

I wonder if everyone has a book in them, some incredible story that is waiting for the right moment to be told. The truth is that I have thought throughout my life that there had to be a book in there somewhere—several books, perhaps, or maybe a whole library.

Lisa Grove-Raider:

How do you describe someone who was born to be a leader right out of the womb? We all know those people who just seem to radiate goodness, who draw people to them, who touch the lives of everyone they meet. My husband, Steven Michael Grove, was one of them. He had an infectious personality; he could make you laugh in any situation. He was undoubtedly one of the most caring people I've ever known. He gave more of himself than he really had to give: his motto was always to help others before he helped himself. He was always working on something or other, always had a project. He did a tremendous amount of community outreach, as well. Steve participated in many different organizations, such as Boy Scouts of America, United Synagogue Youth (USY), The National Kidney Foundation, and The Jewish Home for the Aged, among others. He was the kind of person who would bring people together. He saw life with a glass-half-full attitude and always tried to make people smile.

And when he got sick, he kept on trying to make everyone feel better. He rarely let us in on what was going on his head, or his body for that matter. He was so strong, so reliable, that I believed him when he said, "I'm just fine, really. I'm okay. You don't need to worry about me!" I was truly convinced that he would beat cancer, that he would be one of the survivors—that he would be just fine, like he said. As I was slowly processing my grief, some years later, it was a rare blessing to find the journal he had kept in his final years. Steve's diary was eye-opening. It showed new sides of him; it gave us insight into what he felt and thought as he was going through an enormous amount of suffering.

Steve's journal holds more than his experiences with battling cancer: it holds the lessons of a life well-lived, with all its joys and treasures. There is no guide or handbook on life. But my husband's journey can teach us to face hardships head on. It can inspire us to embrace change, to help others, and to seek help—even born leaders need support. Steve's writing gave our family the gift of a deeper understanding of this extraordinary husband, father, and friend. Sharing his story with others is a way of passing this gift on.

Josh Grove:

When my father was first diagnosed with cancer, I was not seven years old yet. Going through all of this at such a young age was confusing and scary. As you can imagine, I did not really understand the severity of it all. I simply tried to adapt to the situation; my father's disease, medical appointments, treatments and recovery periods simply became part of the new normal for me. Looking back on it now, over twenty years later, reality has set in and I have had time to process everything that my family went through during those years. I also had the incredible privilege of reading my father's reminiscences of that time, see what he made of it all, and understand him a bit better. Therefore, I decided to put this book together to give others the chance to hear his story firsthand. But I also wanted to document my own journey in coming to terms with his death. It's a long process, but healing does come eventually. To anyone who reads this, if you are going through a tough time, I hope this book provides some advice and guidance.

Scott Grove:

My brother Steve was a complicated man. Josh has done a great job in this book of fulfilling Steve's dream of writing a book. Josh's Mother, Lisa revisits her time with Steve eloquently and lovingly. But to fully understand Steve, we have to go a bit deeper. I'm going to talk about the part of Steve that no one really knew, or took the time to understand, not even Steve himself. You see, Steve was gay. He came out to Lisa a mere 10 months before he died. Josh only recently found out, over fifteen years later. I knew my whole life.

Steve grew up in the '60s and '70s, during a time when boys wore blue, played sports, and rode bikes. Girls wore pink, played with dolls, and had tea parties. Steve never really did those "boy" things. He loved music and playing piano. This was a time when words like "fagg*t" and "queer" were used as commonly as "cat" and "dog," and

6

nobody thought twice about it. In fact, Steve's uncles called each other those names as a joke. In the '70s, that was pretty much the norm. To a young boy who was beginning to question his sexuality and who did not know how he fit within society's gender norms, it was unnerving.

Imagine you don't even know you are struggling with your identity because, well, it's just not a thing people around you are openly talking about. Boys were boys and girls were girls. If you were a boy, you were supposed to like girls, and vice versa. Imagine what the world was like for someone who didn't feel like that. On top of this, we had the most unusual of lives growing up—lives marred by tragedy, divorced parents, custody issues, and parents who couldn't stand each other. It was not an easy life.

Yet, this was Steve. He was a survivor. As Steve started growing into his teens, he did his thing. He became a great piano player, made Eagle Scout in the Boy Scouts at an early age and ultimately became Scoutmaster in his Boy Scout troop. After putting himself through school, he started to really do things he enjoyed. He became a magician and put on shows, learned how to play the accordion. And he also volunteered as a youth advisor in a Jewish youth group. This is how he met Lisa.

Lisa Grove-Raider:

Steve and I first met through an organization called United Synagogue Youth, or USY for short. USY empowers Jewish youth within the conservative movement, serving as a platform for them to acquire leadership and team-building skills, fostering friendships, and cultivating a sense of belonging. Both Steve and I participated in social activities, weekend trips, and various other events organized by USY during our teenage years. When I first crossed paths with him, he was already the Director of a Boy Scout camp known as Camp Sequassen in Northwest Connecticut. Even then, it was crystal clear to me that Steve was a born leader. As time passed, our paths continued to intertwine, and we both assumed leadership roles. My respect for Steve continued to grow. It was obvious that those who worked with him held him in high esteem; the younger teens he mentored looked up to him; he was a great networker and knew how to galvanize his peers. Indeed, the roles that were most attractive to Steve were the ones that presented him with the best opportunity to lead by example and make a difference in people's lives.

7

Steve quickly started advancing to top-level roles within the organizations he was a part of. Even my parents, Peter and Sandy Patten, who joined our USY weekend trips as chaperones, developed a deep affection for Steve. They treated him like a son and had the privilege of witnessing his leadership firsthand. After I started working on this book, my mother told me, "We got to see both you and Steve thrive as leaders. It was one of the main reasons you gravitated to one another."

As Steve got older, he started to get involved in new things but worked tirelessly to stay involved and keep ties with each of the organizations he had been a part of. However, disaster soon struck: Steve was diagnosed with cancer. This changed all of our lives.

When you're in love, you feel like you'd do anything for that person, right? You'd go against any obstacle. That's exactly how I felt at the time; I did everything I could to support my husband. However, looking back, I often feel that I let him down. Deep down, I knew Steve was struggling, but I chose to bury those thoughts. Since he wasn't the best at expressing his feelings – he never talked about how much he was suffering with me, and certainly not with our son, Josh – I accepted this and hoped for the best. While he meticulously kept track of his treatments, drug trials, and the latest advances in colon cancer, I turned a blind eye to it all and carried on with our day-to-day lives. I did my best to stand by his side and expressed my love in any way I knew how. What else could I do?

The mounting stress was palpable, but I felt helpless. I could only push so far and never quite managed to get him to talk about how he felt about living with the dreadful disease that claimed his life too soon. In his final moments, a hospice nurse tried to encourage him to talk to a social worker who could offer guidance on how to discuss his illness with Josh. But he never got the chance to do this. He passed away the very next day. Instead, he poured his feelings into his journal, which we've transformed into this book. You'll hear directly from Steve about how he felt and coped with it all.

In a strange way, Steve had an even greater impact on Josh and me in his death than he did while he was alive. He was the reason we started getting involved in cancer charities and tried to help other sufferers; Josh especially made it a priority in his life to be a part of this community. After reliving it all again, twenty years later, I wish I could have done more for Steve. I wish I would have insisted he talk to someone3 about what he was going through. So I encourage you, whatever path you are currently on or whatever hardships you are facing, don't bury your feelings. Don't keep your family in the dark about what you are going through. Don't try to push your worries out of your mind, but acknowledge and share them. If you want to help yourself and your loved ones, staying silent and relying on only yourself is not an option. Always remember that it's okay to talk about your feelings. Reach out to a therapist. Reach out to role models in your life and community or spiritual leaders you look up to. Reach out to your friends and family. It doesn't matter which route you take; the important thing is not to go through it alone.

As we embark on this journey together, you will hear from many people in Steve's life, including my son, Josh. His perspective is unique in that it is written as an adult looking back at his father's life. For Josh, writing this book was a cathartic process, offering him a way to openly express and come to terms with his feelings about his father's death. It was also a way for him to really get to know the father he never really knew. His perspective is one of exploration, as in interacting with Steve through his writing and engaging with stories from people who knew Steve, he came to realize just how many similarities they share. I am so, so proud of the journey Josh chose to undertake by writing this book and bringing his father's words to life.

Josh has done a tremendous amount of work on himself, and I believe that, with time and a lot of hard effort on his part, he has come to terms with his father's death. If you, too, are going through a difficult period in your life, my reminder to you is – to paraphrase Gloria Gaynor – *you will survive*.

Josh Grove:

Many people who knew my father were greatly affected by his passing and were eager to share their stories with me when I contacted them some 16–18 years later. All have their own perspectives and recollections. Just as you have heard from my mother and uncle, you will hear from a variety of people with different backgrounds and connections to my father. It's up to you how you interpret them and what you make of them.

You will get the opportunity to hear Steve's story: how he dealt with his condition firsthand, and how it affected the people around him. At the same time, cancer really can be a relatively sensitive topic, so I threw in some comedic relief and milestone moments. I also wanted to give people advice and opinions, life lessons, stories that they can relate to. But why do all this? Why undertake this difficult journey?

There are certain topics few people are willing to talk about. When it comes to cancer, not many people are willing to engage with the topic, and when they do it is often coated in euphemism or palatable half-truths. My aim was not only to live out my father's dream of getting a book published but to help people by telling his story, as my family and I lived it. So, as you read this, consider the how-tos and the how-not-tos, but also understand the overall goal of this book: to provide a first-hand account of what life with cancer is like from someone who eventually succumbed to it, but also from the perspective of those who were left behind. To tell the truth.

Chapter 1: The Story That Could Have Been

Josh Grove:

As you will hear a lot from me about my father, I thought it would not only be fitting, but necessary for you to hear from the one person who was a part of Steve's life since he was born, his younger brother Scott. Scott watched my father become a man, go to college, get married, build a career, and have a child, all without showing any signs of inner struggle. But Scott knew Steve better than most: he knew that Steve concealing his struggles did not mean he wasn't facing any. Scott's perspective gives you a better idea of who my father was, what he really stood for, and the demons he wrestled with from a young age.

Scott Grove:

My brother Steve was the oldest of us three; he was nine years older than I was, while the middle child – our sister Lisa – was my elder by five years. As I mentioned earlier, Steve's struggle to come to terms with his sexuality weighed especially heavily on him. That was hard enough for a teenage boy to deal with, but soon, things would get even more difficult.

When I was nine years old and Steve was eighteen, our sister Lisa died unexpectedly at age fourteen. It was a heart aneurysm that burst. It was a rough twenty-four-plus hours in our house watching her be in so much pain. We took multiple trips to the hospital, and no one could identify the real issue. There was a major malpractice suit years later that went nowhere; no doctor would testify. My worst memory of it is our father yelling, "She's cold, she's blue, I can't wake her!" Steve ran in and, using his Eagle Scout training, performed CPR on her while we waited for the paramedics to arrive. Eventually, she was taken to the hospital, but our parents came back from their last hospital trip quickly: our sister had died during the night.

So, imagine you are Steve. You've jokingly been called a "faggot" your whole life because you played the piano and were in the Boy Scouts. And now, you've just turned eighteen and your sister dies. Steve's world was crumbling. This was July 1981. Then, in January of 1982, our father sat Steve and me down in the basement and told us that he and our mother were getting a divorce. In retrospect, the divorce was not a completely surprising turn of events—I know now that the loss of a child causes many marriages to fall apart. But at the time I wasn't even ten years old yet, so I didn't understand too much about what was happening. Steve, he was eighteen. It struck him hard. Steve had a big heart, a great sense of humor, and a caring spirit. Lisa's death took a big chunk of that spirit away. And our parents' divorce, on top of other events and life circumstances, continued to erode his generous spirit.

By now, Steve was entering his freshman year of college, which was supposed to be a time of excitement, and in my mind, the time when my brother would have the freedom to discover and come to terms with who he really was. He never got that chance. In hindsight, I wish Steve had been able to go away to college, find like-minded people, figure out who he is, and become OK with it. That being said, my nephew, Josh, is the greatest gift in my life outside my own children so, in that respect, I'm pretty happy Steve chose to go a different route.

But let me continue from where I left off. To say our parents' divorce was a mess would be a major understatement. Our mother (Bonnie), who would ultimately die from issues related to dementia, was incredibly angry. And this was not just anger about the marriage; this was the deep, hurtful anger of burying your only daughter way too early. Our father (Dennis) just wanted things over, so he agreed to our mother's terms. He left with pretty much just his clothes and a lot of bills. Steve had to live at home, work, and try to put himself through school, which was pretty normal for someone his age at the time. What made it not normal was Bonnie. She was so angry at our father that she took every opportunity to turn us kids against him. When I called her in 2012 to tell her our dad had suddenly died, she said, "Finally!" This was almost forty years after their divorce. To my mind, what she did to Steve was awful. She worked day and night to paint our father as a monster, which was so far from the truth.

My dad eventually remarried within a year or two of their divorce, and Steve was the best man at his wedding. Things seemed to normalize a bit for a while, I guess. Again, I was eleven, so I really had no clue what was happening. At that time, my father was living in a one-bedroom apartment across town. He couldn't afford any furniture; he had a folding table, two chairs, and a bed. My brother was struggling to make ends meet, and my mother, well, she blamed all problems on our dad—I wouldn't be surprised if she held my father responsible for Watergate. Steve needed help with car insurance, and my father couldn't help because he had no money. Bonnie, of course, made my dad seem like a millionaire and kept telling Steve that my dad was spending all his money on his "new" family. This was not true, but my brother was so mixed up inside that he eventually fell for my mother's lies.

Steve stopped talking to our father. It seemed to happen overnight: one day he woke up and kicked him out of his life. He never told him why, never accepted a phone call from him, and when our dad would send him cards, Steve (or, to be honest, our mom) just wrote "Return to sender" and put them back in the mail. Steve needed all the family support he could get, and instead, he was unknowingly isolating himself further. I'm guessing at this time in his life Steve was becoming more aware of his sexuality; I could tell that words like "faggot" and "queer" were hurtful to him. I know that confusion and pain played a part in him being susceptible to our mother's influence. I just wish he had talked to our dad about it and got to know the true story, not the one he was getting from Bonnie.

Steve eventually put himself through school and met Lisa through United Synagogue Youth. This was still the '80s, and the world was not very accepting of gay people. There was also no internet, so it was also harder to be exposed to new ideas or meet like-minded individuals. By the time Steve had met Lisa, he had learned to operate within the confines of the societal norms that he had been taught. He did what he needed to do to survive; he put up walls around the pain and discomfort of growing up as a gay man. He was never able to fully comprehend his sexuality, let alone live it out.

My brother compartmentalized a lot of his feelings and avoided situations and people that made him confront his painful inner struggle. That, at times, included me. I was a reminder of our sister, of our old family drama, and on top of that, I had a wonderful relationship with our father. He distanced himself from me; it's what he needed to do at the time, I think. At the same time, he turned outward and became everything to everybody who never really knew him. He became a great leader in the Scouts, USY, and his community, and people would heap praise on him for how kind and giving he was. See, strangers would never get close enough to really get to know him or his inner struggles, so he invested his care and affection in them because it was safer that way.

So that was how he lived. He married Lisa and lived the typical family life. They bought a home, upgraded to a bigger one, and raised Josh. They wanted another child badly, but after years of trying all kinds of things, even considering adoption, they gave up. This turned out to be a blessing given that at the age of 37 he was diagnosed with colon cancer.

As you read this book, I'm sure you will come to see Steve as a wonderful man whose life was cut tragically short. He accomplished great things and cared deeply for people. You will read that, when people would come to visit Steve when he was sick, he would steer the conversation towards them instead. Josh interprets this as Steve displaying selflessness. I see it differently. That wasn't out of kindness; it was out of an instinct for survival. My brother didn't want to dig into himself too deeply. He didn't want to let anyone in. The stories you will read about how great he was to people are all true. But he did it for people who never knew him. Me? He never really embraced a relationship with me. While it was awful for me – he was my big brother, after all – as I write this, I do understand why he did this. I was a reminder of all the pain he lived through. I knew who he was; no one else did.

Just before he died, my brother finally came to terms with his sexuality and began living the life he had denied himself. By that time, it had become more socially acceptable to do so. The tragedy? He only ever came out to Lisa. I knew the moment she said, "I have something to tell you." I could have told you when I was fifteen years old that my brother was gay; I only wish I had known enough then to help him.

I was thirty-one years old when Steve died. I got a chance to talk to him a week or so before he passed away. It was like all of our other conversations: superficial. We never talked about the demons he had fought his whole life, never discussed the important things, which is something I have to live with to this day. I used to be a part of a family of five: two married parents, and three kids, of which I was the youngest. On the day that my sister died, in July of 1981, that family got torn apart, and it never recovered. Steve never recovered, our mother got worse over the years, and our father had to resign himself not only to losing his daughter but also to his son never talking to him again. My father, Dennis, passed away in 2012, and he never got a chance to talk to his son before Steve's death.

When Steve died, I did what I consider my biggest mitzvah in life. I quietly and subtly brought my father back into Lisa and Josh's life. He immediately became Josh's "pop-pop," and I believe those years he spent by Josh's side, up to my father's death in 2012, helped provide closure for my father: he had missed out on his son's life, but not his grandson's. Josh and my dad had a special bond because of Steve. Josh probably didn't understand it until he got older, but that relationship, for my father, was not just a relationship with Josh; it was with Steve, too.

I know if Steve had survived cancer and had been able to live his life as an openly gay adult, a lot of the interpersonal issues he had dealt with his entire life would have been resolved—his relationship with our father, with me, you name it. It's such a tragedy: "Steve Grove, the story that could have been."

There are many lessons you can take from this book, and I'm sure Josh will do a great job in guiding you through them. Josh didn't even make it to his eleventh birthday with his father alive, yet he has understood everything that was good about Steve. I hope this story is as much a lesson in living life to you as it is to Josh. From my side, I encourage you to remember just one thing: you only live once, so treat every single day as if it were your last. Don't ever let any rules or prevailing societal norms dictate how you should live your life. The world is accepting of anything you want to be. Don't be Steve. Don't die with half a heart deadened by tragedy and sadness.

Chapter 2: The First Signs of Trouble

Josh Grove:

My father always had his sights on what came next; he always had a goal, a plan, something he was working on. Yet sometimes life throws you a curveball that puts everything else on hold, something that throws into question the very foundations of who you are and how you operate as a person. For my father, this moment came in the summer of 2000.

Steve Grove:

When I was told I was sick, I went looking for a book of answers. I went looking for a book written by someone who could tell me what the steps were, someone who could tell me what I should feel and what I should do. You see, I am an accountant. Yes, a boring accountant who believes that everything has an order. In science, we have step one, step two, and so on... I remember in high school when I used to take hydrochloric acid and baking soda, put it in a balloon, and see that the reaction is the same each time. There were steps; there was an order in which to do things; things worked in a certain manner. Well, guess what? When you get cancer, that order goes out the window. Your life is turned upside down. And you have to go along with it. There isn't much that you can do but roll with the punches.

Josh Grove:

When my father was first diagnosed, you can imagine it threw him for a loop. Cancer can change the way you think: you can go from a glass half full to a glass half empty in the blink of an eye. But Steve had a never-give-up mentality. He was determined to beat it, and this determination is something that stayed with him until the end. Although he felt that getting cancer was very unlucky, he chose not to dwell on it. He did not panic; he did not get sad. But he did become frustrated—the type of frustration that you can't quite put your finger on. This was the savage irony of it all. Steve was – it is hard to think about this – still quite young at the time. He was finally figuring out who he was when he got the devastating news.

But I am getting ahead of myself. In June 2000, Steve had not yet been diagnosed. It was when the first signs of trouble started appearing.

Steve Grove:

I was terribly lucky to have symptoms show up in the form of pain. It took a few tests to determine that I had colon cancer, but on June 24, 2000, cancer was the farthest thing from our minds.

I woke up after a few days of indigestion and told my wife I didn't feel well. I had some localized pain in my upper left abdomen and had this terrible, sick feeling in my gut. We were in the midst of moving our entire lives out to the beach to spend a week with Lisa's cousins and their kids. We had rented a small beach cottage in Old Lyme, Connecticut, and this was going to be a well-deserved vacation after the year we had just had. The house was loaded with boxes, suitcases, and bags ready to be packed into our two vans, including bicycles, lawn chairs... you name it, we were taking it with us. However, I didn't feel well, so I sent Lisa on her way and went up to see my friend Harry Schwartz.

Harry was a GI Doctor at Griffin Hospital, which is located in Derby, Connecticut. It was a Saturday in the holiday season, and I knew that if I went to any large hospital, I would be there all day and never get looked at, so I called Harry. Luckily, he was on call. I went up to Griffin for the day. He looked at me and felt around and was mystified. Pulled muscle, infection, perhaps diverticulitis, he thought. He did a few tests. Nothing showed up on the blood test, so he decided to send me for a CAT scan.

Now here is something I found out that day: what medical professionals tell you can be quite different from the reality. I had not eaten anything that day, was feeling lousy, and was asked to drink this white fluid they called contrast. I asked what it was, and they told me that I would drink a pint now, and then another pint in an hour, and then the CAT Scan would be able to pick up more of what was going on. Let me warn you now: they have called it the wrong thing. They need to rename it Yuck in a Bottle. That is all it is. They make a feeble attempt to try to improve the taste by putting something sweet into it, and trust me, that only makes it worse. Most of the time, you are drinking this stuff on an empty stomach and there are no directions on how to do it. They just tell you to drink it down and that it may taste a bit bitter. Bitter?! Bitter??? That is like calling a hurricane a light rainstorm.

There needs to be the following label on the bottle:

- *Try and ignore the thick, rotten-milk look.*

- *This stuff tastes terrible, and you're going to gag.*

- *You're going to feel worse after you drink it.*

- *It is masked with sweeteners, which makes it taste even worse.*

- *You will never want to look at this stuff again.*

- *Once more, with feeling: you're going to feel worse after you drink it.*

I had to laugh when they asked me how it went down. I was tempted to say, "Well, if I choose between layer cake and contrast at my next party, I will be sure to select contrast!" The stuff is awful, and you can only drink it fast and hope that it stays where it is supposed to be. If you've ever had the "pleasure" of drinking it and have wanted to immediately spew it all out, just know that you are not alone.

Lisa Grove-Raider:

You can understand from Steve's account that this process is no walk in the park. However, there is a reason you are having that procedure. There is a bigger picture to keep in mind here, which is how we should all look at these stories. Having more of a macro viewpoint can work wonders with keeping your mind at ease in the moment.

Josh Grove:

Steve was pragmatic and matter-of-fact in his descriptions. He told it like it was. He was not going to sugarcoat a difficult situation just to paint a rosy picture for others. He believed he could help people best by being honest, not by giving them a false sense of hope. For instance, I remember that, whenever someone would walk into his hospital room, he was thankful; at the same time, he let them know that he knew exactly why they were there. He knew they would not be visiting if what he was going through was not serious. Some would call that harsh. I, however, cannot help but admire it.

My friends and family have always joked about me being a straight shooter: they have told me I can be extremely blunt sometimes. As I got older, I started to discover and perfect my strengths while working on my weaknesses. I tried to be more understanding, more compassionate, but also to never shy away from the harsh truths of life. This, too, is something I share with my father. Similar to his way of thinking, I believe living in honesty, being at ease with difficult truths, is a better way to live your life. The cliche phrase *the truth will set you free* is tremendously applicable here. Whether it's a work situation or a personal one, being able to wrestle with the truth by creating an action plan, both short-term and long-term, can help you create a better pathway for yourself.

Of course, understanding and accepting the harsh truths in life are two completely different things. The realization that you have cancer is not easy to swallow. Accepting that a large part of your life from now on will be spent in hospitals or undergoing various medical tests and procedures is difficult. But this understanding and acceptance will help you become a more well-rounded person. My father always said to me growing up: "Something good can always come out of something bad." I know that, taken at face value, this is a cliche statement. However, it is true. It was true for my father at the time of battling this disease, and it has been true for me, then and throughout my life.

A good friend of mine from high school, Andrew Chasanoff, who has been a big part of my life since, once told me: "Josh, you never want to change your goal, because you set your sights on attaining that goal for a reason. What you can do is change your plan. A plan is malleable and adaptable to your life. It's a matter of how you pivot to the next step of the plan." If there is one single piece of advice I can give you, it is this: "Never change the goal. Change the plan." This motto has shaped who I am now, and I firmly believe that, if my father were here today, he would fully stand by it because that is the way he lived his life, too.

My father's overarching goal becomes transparent in the pages of his journal and never changes throughout. It is always: to beat cancer. The plan, however, would change according to new information that came his way or new treatments that the doctors would suggest. It is clear from the excerpt above that he dealt with things as they came, focusing on one thing at a time. Now, this test. Now, this procedure. Now, this treatment. At the end of the day, he knew that having cancer was out of his control, so instead he focused on controlling the controllable, on setting achievable goals. He was always forward-thinking, but remained realistic in his goal-setting and plan-making.

Sitting down and designing attainable goals for yourself is not a flashy job, nor should it be; it is a matter of resolve. The key word here is "attainable." Setting realistic benchmarks for yourself is particularly important. This can help you attain your goals at a much faster pace. Do not worry so much about the end goal, but rather, stay focused on the journey. There will be many steps before you get where you want to be; give each step your full attention. Ultimately, if you continually check off the boxes as you go along, you are putting yourself in a better situation. Getting yourself from your current state to a better, future state involves an immense amount of patience and perseverance. Do it. Your future self will thank you for it. Stay true to yourself and you will be able to recognize the truth of what you truly want to accomplish. You will find your "Why?" Why am I doing this? What is the purpose behind my actions?

My father wrote these stories down to paint a realistic picture of what was going on in his body, as well as in his head, along with how it affected the people around him. He hoped that reading about the ins and outs of his battle with cancer and cancer treatments would be helpful to others going through the same thing. But I would go one step further and say that the way in which he faced this battle, taking it step by step, procedure by procedure, can be a valuable lesson to us all, not just those suffering from cancer.

Steve Grove:

I had a CAT Scan, but before I did, the tech asked me if I had any other medical problems. Now, here is another very important thing. When it comes to your own care, SPEAK UP. I did mention that I had a kidney disorder and she thanked me for telling her. She was injecting me with some dye to add "more contrast" for the CAT scan. I asked if I was going to glow when this was over, and she told me only when I got close to high power lines. She was very nice, but at that moment it didn't strike me as very funny.

The dye they use has two versions. A super and a mild version. It's kind of like selecting your salsa—mild or hot. I selected the mild version due to my kidneys, and off we went. It felt like someone was pouring hot soup into my veins, and after eight hours of no food, and then drinking this contrast, you can just about imagine how I felt while lying on that table.

Later in the afternoon, Dr. Schwartz came back and confirmed that he and the radiologist found a small case of diverticulitis and would start treating it as such. He put me on some medicine and sent me home. I would rest a few days, relax, and then be good as new, I thought. After a few days on the medicine, I was feeling better—not perfect, but enough to get out of bed, go to the beach, and enjoy my family for a few days. The month of July went on, but the pain kept coming back each time Dr. Schwartz tried to take me off the medicine, so we decided that we needed to get a look in there.

When he explained what exactly he meant by that, I wasn't that keen anymore. I believe my exact words were: "You're going to do WHAT?"

Chapter 3: A Colonoscopy and a Diagnosis

Steve Grove:

I remember listening to my dear friend and doctor, Harry Schwartz, and saying to him, "You're going to do WHAT? What is it you are going to do?" I know that thousands of people have this procedure every day, but it doesn't mean that it's for everyone. Each time he took me off the various medications I was taking, I managed to both lose some weight and also have the pain reappear. He was concerned and wanted to move ahead with the procedure: a colonoscopy.

One of the things that they ask you to do before this procedure is to buy a little three-ounce bottle in the store and drink it the afternoon before you come in. This is meant to cleanse you out.

Let me tell you what that means... Or in other words, let me tell you the real label they should put on this stuff:

- *Eat nothing for five days prior to drinking this stuff.*
- *They've added a sweetener for the taste, but this does nothing.*
- *You're going to hate drinking this.*
- *Stay close to the bathroom afterward.*
- *You better have a personal bathroom.*
- *No one gets between you and the bathroom at that time.*
- *You won't believe what will happen next.*
- *You would never believe you can be so well cleaned out on the inside.*
- *This "cleaning" will last well into the next day.*
- *For the rest of your life, you'll shudder when you see this product on the shelf in the supermarket.*

There is a market for this stuff and there is a lot of it sold. I could not believe what that stuff did to me in a short period of time. I had not eaten much, so it was not too bad, but trust me, you'll know what I am talking about if you ever have to drink this stuff. As I was going through this procedure, I wondered what kind of comedy routine this would make for Jay Leno or David Letterman. I wonder if I will get a chance to find out.

Josh Grove:

I, too, have had a colonoscopy; actually, I've had several. When I was 24 years old, I had my first one and I was really glad I did, but I'll get to that later. I remember having to drink that liquid twenty-four hours before my procedure and just how bad it was—not drinking it, but the effect it had. The taste has gotten better from when my father took it, but not much else has changed. I had to stay awfully close to a bathroom the entire time. It was rather uncomfortable, but I knew it was necessary to get accurate results. Following the doctor's orders to a T is something that is also necessary. If or when you ever get a colonoscopy, remember that.

The actual procedure itself is not all that bad, or at least it wasn't for me. They keep you comfortable. There are several doctors present, including the anesthesiologist, to make sure you're relaxed before the procedure. Then you're under anesthesia and wake up in recovery feeling just fine—a little groggy, perhaps, but most surgeries that require anesthesia will make you feel this way. And then you're waiting for the results.

My personal results had several polyps (growths in my colon), all benign. My doctor explained that I am incredibly lucky I did this at an early age. He explained that the activity they saw was fast-growing, which could be a sign of early issues. Thankfully, he finished off by adding that they were all benign, but that I would need to come back for a colonoscopy every year, at least until the growth starts to slow down. Typically, it slows down in five to ten years, in most cases. As I was sitting there listening to him and his team tell me their recommendations and suggestions, I started to think, "Do they have my best interest at heart? Who am I to question it, but is this the best course of action?" After thinking long and hard about this and getting a second opinion from a previous doctor, I believed it was the best thing for my health. I told myself my future self will thank me later.

Lisa Grove-Raider:

How I handled the situation was simply by monitoring Steve's expectations and reacting in ways that would be helpful, staying strong. I knew that the process of getting a diagnosis was affecting Steve way more than it was affecting me, and more than he was letting on. Being a little naive about the whole thing, I still had a blind hope that we were all going to get through it at this point.

Steve Grove:

We got to the hospital on the day of the procedure, and they got me ready. They explained that, somehow, I would be awake, but won't feel the procedure. They even allowed me to lay on my side and watch the procedure live on the monitor.

Now, let me explain something. I am an accountant and not a doctor. I didn't pass chemistry and couldn't stand anatomy. Why would I want to watch any of this stuff on a monitor? I would just rather they put me to sleep, do their thing, and wake me when it's finished. From what I can tell, however, they want you a little awake in this procedure so you can move or shift, or possibly get up and dance the jig... I don't know, but it isn't a heavy drug they give you. In my case, they didn't give me enough and I woke up right up... and they were at about the 75% mark, turning a corner.

Here goes another description of a common medical term: the doctor and nurses told me that I may feel" slight discomfort and/or a little pressure" during the process. Let me tell you what that means in plain English:

- *This is going to hurt.*
- *You are going to be in a lot of pain.*
- *You won't be able to think about anything but the pain.*
- *We call it pressure and discomfort because we've never been through it ourselves.*

I don't mean to be cruel, but I woke up and felt nothing resembling slight discomfort or pressure. It hurt. Plain and simple. I mentioned this to my doctor and he finished up the procedure, although he claimed he had barely looked at 75% of the inside. I recovered from the drugs and managed to get dressed, feeling only the slightest discomfort by now, when the doctor broke the news.

He told us that he had seen a mass inside my colon and had taken several samples of it. It was these samples that had slowed down the procedure, and it was why the medicine had worn off, allowing me to awaken. He apologized and told me that it was quite possible that this mass could be cancer. I half-listened to him, and half-hoped that he was wrong. My wife and I talked about it on the way home. We knew that the lab results would not be in until the following Tuesday. It was a Friday afternoon, and it was going to be a long weekend. The diagnosis was Malignant Adenocarcinoma.

Josh Grove:

Malignant Adenocarcinoma is a term used for diseases in which abnormal cells divide uncontrollably and can invade nearby tissues. Malignant cells can also spread to various parts of your body through the blood and lymph systems. There are many types of malignancy. I won't get into specifics, but I will say that these cells can begin in places like your bone, tissue, and skin. Essentially, they can appear and grow basically anywhere. What this all describes, in a nutshell, is cancer.

I remember exactly where I was when my father was told he had cancer. I had gone to a friend's house after school and stayed there through dinnertime. I remember exactly where I was sitting, too. I was in my friend's basement playing with action figures, waiting for my mom to walk into the house or call with the news. Although I did not fully understand what it meant or what would happen, I knew things were going to change. I remember hearing it in my mother's voice when she called to tell me.

Steve Grove:

The answer was surgery in the next few weeks and then a determination of what had gone on. When they did the surgery, they found the tumor to be two centimeters in size. It had broken through ever so slightly off the wall of the colon. It was in the upper left part, so they only had to take out twelve inches or so. My lymph system was clear; chest, stomach, and most everything was clear. They found some spread to my liver and through examination in surgery, found four to five small nodules sitting on my liver. I don't have liver cancer, they explained, and these small nodules were just sitting in my liver, kind of just hanging out. That's the way it was described to me. These nodules are quite common in this situation and my liver functions were perfect, so we had time and could explore our options.

However, it's pretty heavy to wake up in the hospital and kind of lay there thinking about nothing else other than the fact that this is not over yet. It was almost going to start another life of its own after I got out of the hospital and recovered from the surgery. We met with a wonderful oncologist in the hospital, who explained that he could help us. He said we could deal with these issues using the latest in chemotherapy, and he would talk to us after I got out and felt better. I had an MRI and some blood work so that they could clearly monitor the condition and its progress.

At least we now knew what we were dealing with. If we knew the problem, we could move ahead toward solving it. If I had cancer, we could do something so that I could feel better. For two months, I had dealt with pain and a terrible feeling in my stomach, not to mention a lot of weight loss and loss of appetite. I thought, if it's cancer, tell me now, and let's do something about it. This pain and suffering deal is for the birds.

Chapter 4: Support Networks

Josh Grove:

My father always dreamt of being famous for a day. He always strived to be the best at everything he undertook and wished to make a name for himself, to be remembered. After he passed, he did succeed in this goal, although he was not around to witness it. I was lucky enough to see it, all of it.

Throughout my life, many of his friends and relatives would tell me stories about how my father had impacted them—whether by helping them through a tough time or giving them advice. But it wasn't until I started working on this book that I truly "got it." One part of the journey I undertook in writing this book involved reaching out to various alumni associations that my father had been a part of. These included the Boy Scouts, business organizations, charity organizations, and some United Synagogue social networks. The power of social media brought people to me in droves. After a single post in tandem with one of Steve's friends, I had hundreds of messages flooding my inbox. E-mails, text messages, and phone calls followed. Everyone had a story or anecdote about Steve. Everyone was so eager to speak with me. It was as if they felt they had lost a friend and were regaining him through me. I cannot begin to express the pride and honor I felt in hearing their stories. Some, he had known for many years, some for less than five years. But all shared the same appreciation for Steve. He had touched so many people.

Many told me that Steve had a larger-than-life personality. He wore his heart on his sleeve and shared his humor with everyone around him. But when it came to his illness, he never let anyone in on his worries. He knew that the battle with cancer would be no walk in the park; it would be long, tenuous, exhausting, and tiring. And he did not want others to suffer along with him. There was an external image of himself that he wanted to maintain.

Medical conditions take a toll on the sufferer, but sometimes they can affect the people who are helping them through it even more. Among many of Steve's close friends, there was a consensus that, when Steve was diagnosed with cancer, all he wanted to do is protect his friends and family. As he got closer to the end, he held his cards closer and closer to his chest. He tried to keep people close to him as far away from the disease as he could. Simply put, he did not want to bring people down. Yet, reading through his journal, I could not help but notice the discrepancy between how he had been feeling and the brave face he was putting on for the benefit of his friends and family.

Steve Grove:

The test ended up showing that I had adenocarcinoma – your garden-variety colon cancer – and they were not sure what stage it was in. They could not determine on the CAT scans if it had come through the lining of the colon, but it was a small area, only about two centimeters. So, if it was cancer, there just wasn't a ton of it. The pain that I had was enough to bring attention to it, and now was the time to act. Dr. Schwartz's partner called me and told me the news the following Tuesday. He suggested I get in touch with a surgeon as soon as possible. I just sat back in my chair at my desk. The door to my office was closed, and in that moment, I felt more alone than ever.

As I mentioned earlier, it's not that I hadn't had my share of suffering. Growing up, putting myself through college, starting a business, running a business, building a house, getting married and starting a family, there had been plenty of it. But there are some moments when you feel terribly alone. This is not to say that you feel lonely; it is to say that you feel alone. It is about a singular and personal suffering that is just yours alone to bear. It is not a joint Suffering Project. The pain is yours and there isn't anything that anyone can do about it.

Josh Grove:

The feeling of loneliness is very relatable to me, as I am sure it is for many people. That word has shaped many aspects of my own life; it is a topic I have thought about long and hard. I always felt that loneliness and privacy go hand in hand. I never knew why though. As I grew older, I started to think about this in relation to my father. People have told me that my father was a very outgoing person. However, when it came to his personal life and struggles, he tried to keep that part of himself private. The distinction he makes here is significant: he was not feeling *lonely*, because he was always

28

surrounded by people; but he was feeling *alone*, because no matter how many people we have around us, some things we must deal with on our own.

There was a tremendous amount of pain below the surface with Steve. He was wrestling not just with cancer, but also struggling with his identity, as well as dealing with family issues, financial burdens, and remnants of early trauma. How does a person handle all of that? And what made him able to stay positive and forward-thinking? Was he doing it for himself, or for the people around him? My uncle Scott mentions that he believes this was a mechanism of self-protection on Steve's part, a way for him to avoid traumatic memories and grappling with his inner demons. My mother told me that it was for the benefit of others: even in his final years, Steve tried to make sure his loved ones did not worry. Perhaps it was a little bit of both.

I want to go back in time here for a moment. When Steve was in his older teenage years, his sister Lisa died suddenly of a brain aneurysm—my uncle Scott talked about this earlier. After that event, their family dynamics changed drastically, as is to be expected. Steve, in particular, struggled. Many of his peers, co-workers, friends, and even extended members of his family told me they noticed a change in him after losing his sister at such an early age. Some said it was as though he was carrying the weight of the world on his shoulders, and did not want to let others share in the burden. At the same time, he was also dealing with other issues within his family. Steve and his father did not always see eye to eye. As he grew older, in his high school years and throughout college, their disagreements grew more heated. Steve chose to follow his own path, as did his father. Their family split up. Steve had to put himself through college alone, without any help. A lot of the ways in which Steve coped with his battle with cancer ultimately connect back to early issues with his family. His difficult relationship with his father and the trauma of losing his sister took a major toll on him, as they would on any adolescent. And in dealing with these hardships he developed his strategies for coping, one of which may have been to separate these two parts of his life – his inner struggles from his outgoing persona – in order to shield others from his suffering.

When he was diagnosed with cancer, my father began, in a way, to distance himself. He didn't talk about his illness much or the inner battles he was facing. Later, he stopped communicating about it altogether. It was as if he believed he would simply beat the cancer on his own. I never remember him showing any weakness. Around me and my mom, he always tried to put on a brave face. He would also throw in light comments and use his dry humor to give off a positive vibe. I think it was a "fake it 'til you make it" mentality that helped him cope: he knew that by remaining cheerful he would be better able to endure the pain while, at the same time, he could continue to check off boxes and move forward with treatments.

I talked to one of Steve's best friends growing up, Paul Ryder, about this. He talked about how loyal and protective Steve had always been of his friends and family; he was loyal to a fault and always took it upon himself to cheer them up. This is consistent with what I have heard from others, including my mother. Protecting those closest to him from the harsh realities of the illness was perhaps a manifestation of Steve's ideals and morals, another way in which he enacted the loyalty and protectiveness that Paul mentioned as his character traits.

I can understand and appreciate this. Loyalty is a value I have lived by my entire life; anyone who knows me can confirm that it is a belief that I hold deeply and that characterizes all of my personal relationships. But I also think one must find a balance. It is one thing to be loyal to your friends and family; it is quite another to put everyone and everything before your own needs. How can you ask for help if you are always worrying about shielding others from your own suffering? In the prologue, my mother wrote that she had not been aware of the stress and weight that my father carried within him throughout this period: "*When you are used to someone who is always so strong and reliable, you believe them when they tell you, 'I'm good, really, I'm okay!'*" But Steve was not okay; the disease was starting to take a toll.

Steve Grove:

You just feel alone. Where do you turn? Who do you tell? (…) I am sure that, if you have to endure chemotherapy, you know that there are side effects. I am amazed, however, that the drugs I was taking had me feeling so much worse at times than the pain it was supposed to be taking care of. You take all of these medications that then give you other problems. The medical community always refers to these as "temporary conditions." Well, they are not temporary when you are having these problems.

Josh Grove:

It is clear from these passages how much my father was struggling, but his family and friends did not realize this at the time. The phrase "up the creek without a paddle" references an old creek located in Portsmouth Harbor in England, and relates to a sense of hopelessness, of feeling trapped or stuck. This image of a lone canoeist, trying to move forward with no way of paddling, came to mind when I read my father's words. How difficult and alienating it must have been to face all those different struggles and not talk about them!

Yet while my father did not share his worries about the cancer, he *did* realize how important it was to have people around you to help you through. He turned to his support network for comfort; he took pleasure in simple things like spending time with them and hugging them. This may seem like a contradiction, but I don't believe that it is. It is simply a separation of those parts of his life he found difficult to talk about, such as the physical effects of his illness or the financial difficulties he mentions later. Though he always maintained a cheery façade and did not let on how much he was struggling, throughout his journal, he also stressed the importance of human touch and personal connections, including in the medical setting, with the nursing personnel that took care of him.

Steve Grove:

Something good can always come out of something bad. So many people have reached out and have come to see me that I haven't seen in months, or even years! In some cases, people got in touch who I never would have thought would do so.

(...) Loving others will help. Show your love for others and others will show this back. It's hard to express in words how much hugging helps you feel. Even at moments when you least feel like being happy, a hug will erase any bad thoughts that you may have. Human touch and contact are very important in the entire recovery process. This is the reason our whole medical system is screwed up. By not having enough nurses these days, we delay a whole step in the healing process. The nursing process isn't just one of physical

31

recuperation. It is also one of emotional healing and support. They go hand in hand.

Josh Grove:

The feeling of loneliness is a heavy burden to bear. But when you open the door to others, that weight is lessened. Sharing the burden is a crucial part of the healing process.

Steve Grove:

How do you break this news to your family, friends, and loved ones? I thought a lot about how to do this and decided it was best to just come right out and say it. I think it is vitally important that you are honest and open with people who love you. It is very difficult to discuss these matters because there are just so many questions. But giving others information will help you in the end. The key to this part is to believe in what you are telling people. If good things happen, you'll be happy to talk about them and hear yourself sharing them. Although questions may still abound in your mind, talking will help and heal you.

At times, of course, you will be tired of talking about your condition. You will get tired of breaking the news and going over the facts again and again. You'll find yourself not wanting to talk to others, and that's okay. You'll want to curl up and pull back. We have caller ID on our phones and a phone answering machine. There were many times that we just let the machine pick up our calls and listened to the messages afterwards. I managed to get back to people over the following weeks, but it was in my own time and when I felt like talking. People are all well-meaning, and I do believe it's a good idea to tell people and keep them informed.

Josh Grove:

We all have moments when we want a reprieve from the views or presence of others. Needing time alone (wanting to "curl up and pull back," as my father puts it) can be healthy as long as there is a purpose. But we must remember to let others back in. Having close friends and family by your side when you are feeling lonely can be a huge source of comfort.

Start looking around you. Figure out who truly is in your personal support system—the group of people who have similar values to you, similar interests, and most importantly, ideals. Do you have people who are loyal to you and vice versa? Have you built a support network for when things get tough? If not, start building one. Look among your family and friends; look among your communities, or the organizations you are part of; make new connections. This will not only help ease feelings of loneliness, but give you strength to move forwards, better yourself, achieve your goals, and face difficulties when they arise. Even if you are not going through a difficult time right now, do it: whatever connections or support you will take away from this process will be more than you had coming in.

One thing my father was exceptionally good at was acknowledging that his family and friends were always by his side throughout this long ordeal. He truly valued all the relationships he had built. Many of those who were close to him have shared with me stories and moments in which they were affected by something Steve said or did. He was someone who always tried to entertain people, but at the same time he was there for them at a moment's notice. And he truly valued being a part of that support network for so many people. He struggled with it at times, of course—as is only human. He had moments when he turned inwards. But in the end, he realized it was important to keep connecting with others, even if your first impulse is to keep them at arm's length:

Steve Grove:

Not much else matters when you are told you have cancer other than the question of your own mortality. You now know there is something inside you that can mean the end of you. This may sound harsh, but it's the truth and you'll feel this way.

The start is a tough place to be. It is where everything is running through your head. What should I do first? Who do I call first? Why do I have to call and tell everyone? Why can't I just lay here and suffer on my own? Well... you can't. Whether or not you realize it, your attitude will be what holds up the rest of the world. It becomes an amazing, almost impossible feat. You have to hold everyone up when you are least feeling able to. Trust me: there isn't any other way.

Josh Grove:

"Why can't I just lay here and suffer on my own?" That is the question my father asked himself. And he soon came to the conclusion that this was not a helpful attitude. He realized that it was important to reach out to your support network, to find comfort in others, to not turn away from the world. When life's burdens get too hard to bear, the impulse to crawl inwards is strong, but must be fought.

Being diagnosed with cancer is not something I have gone through, of course. It is a rude awakening: as my father mentions above, you are quite abruptly faced with your own mortality. Yet isn't this something we all must do at one point? Whether it is through a bout of illness, the death of a parent, or simply due to the natural process of aging, we all have to face our own mortality sooner or later, and it is something we must, by necessity, face alone. But in facing it, we do not have to cut ourselves off from those we love—or, as my father so eloquently put it: *alone* should not mean *lonely*.

Chapter 5: Moving Forward, Standing Still

Josh Grove:

Every human being has the capacity for growth and change; indeed, what is life if not a state of continual change? My father was also a big believer in this. In spite – or perhaps because – of the terminal illness he knew he had, in his journal he wrote repeatedly about the importance of being forward-thinking, of continuing to grow as a person, of becoming stronger through hardship. Yet, if you had asked my father what life was all about, I am not sure that is the part he would choose to focus on. His answer would probably be something along the lines of, "Life is about cherishing the memories we make and enjoying the people around us." I don't believe there is a contradiction there. It is clear from his journal that Steve was the kind of rare person who could do both: look to the future, but also take the time to stand still and appreciate good things and good people when they came along; while he was a relentless optimist who liked to plan ahead and set himself goals for the future, he knew when it was time to stop and smell the roses.

Steve Grove:

We meet many people in life. With some, we come together to make up what we call a community. But each of us comes from a different background. What makes some people very rich and others very poor has often puzzled me. And after I was struck with cancer, I thought a lot about why some people are sick and others remain healthy their entire lives. I wondered why some have no challenges in their lives – or so it would seem – while others must face challenge after challenge.

In many ways, it's just plain old luck. One of my friends used to refer to life as the "lucky or unlucky sperm club," which sounds pretty vague, but it does have meaning. It refers to the family we are born into. In our lives, many things go on to shape who and what we are. The amount and type of struggle we face has got to have an effect on the way in which we approach and manage our lives. And a lot of it starts with our family and upbringing. Being raised by parents who can put their children in the best of schools has got to be a very different existence than growing up in a family that has always had to save and scrimp on everything. Yet money is not the key to happiness, nor is it necessarily a gift, though it can provide a certain freedom from stress. In fact, after all my years as an accountant, I clearly see how money can be a curse. Struggle makes you stronger. If you are able to face life with all of its stresses, to forge a way ahead despite the obstacles, I have to believe that there is some meaning to be found there. Something born out of hardship.

I know that some will disagree. My wife and I have close friends who have been severely tested in their lives—their children have had problems; they have faced all sorts of difficulties; they have lived through struggle after struggle. And I dare say it would be hard to convince them that good things come from the struggle. Mrs. X is one such friend. She says that it may be true that "the Lord only gives us the challenges that we can handle," but she would also like to know why we can't have one thing at a time to deal with.

We have laughed about it often. She has told me that someday she is going to have a talk with the Almighty One and ask Him a few questions. She is religious and faithful, and yet still feels she has been tested excessively. I told her that we can't ask why; the answer is just "because" and that will have to be enough. Our shoulders may feel heavy from burdens at times, but that is usually the time to start holding our heads a little higher and finding a little more inside of us to help us deal with what we have to deal with.

I believe that faith and determination have a lot to do with our personal survival and success. I have no idea how things will end for me at the end of my life in 60 years, but I do know that the cancer I have is curable, and that longevity is in my genes on all sides of my family. Many of my family members lived well into their 90s.

I have so much to say. I don't know if this will ever get published, but I know that I could have used this book on the day I was told I was sick with cancer. It is a book of how-to's that I could not find. It is a book that talks about the funny stories and situations that I went through and my thoughts on them. It tells of my continued treatments and the end of my treatments. It is my hope that this book will help you if you are sick. It is my hope that this book will make you laugh and make you think. I will be honest, however: I started this book before starting the second part of my

36

chemotherapy. I suppose I just have the attitude that I will be fine and that I will beat this awful disease I carry in me.

I want to thank my wife Lisa and my son Joshua Adam, who are the loves of my life. They are real-life heroes who are grappling with this disease on a day-to-day basis: dealing with the phone calls, the fruit baskets, visitors, and flower arrangements coming to our house. They are the ones who have to put up with my exhaustion and occasional bouts of irritation... okay, frequent bouts of irritation. They are here day after day, helping me through this period of time, which seems to stretch into eternity.

I also want to thank all the rest of my family and friends, too numerous to mention, who offered their assistance, whether it was by helping with babysitting, doing yard work, and even staining the deck (my father-in-law stained my deck while I was in the hospital; he did it because he knows I am lousy at this type of thing).

Lastly, I want to thank all of you who are reading this book. Whether you are searching for support, advice or laughter, or need help to get through a difficult time, I hope you find what you are looking for in its pages.

Josh Grove:

Looking back now, one thing that strikes me is the manner in which my father responded to both internal and external stresses. He remained optimistic and forward-thinking when talking about the future, yet also took the time to stop and appreciate the people around him. In these pages, which were intended as a prologue to the journal that Steve hoped would become a book, he wanted to first make sure that everyone who helped him during this difficult period was thanked for it. He did not require thank-yous or accolades himself, but he gave them freely and generously to others. And he stayed humble throughout the entire process. There is a word I believe is apt here, and that is the word *mensch*. If you are not familiar with it, it is a Yiddish word that comes from old English and German and means a person of integrity and honor; someone who puts others before themselves without thinking twice about it. Steve embodied the true meaning of a humble mensch.

This is also the word my mother's only brother, my uncle Marc Patten, used to describe Steve. He would say it often: "Steve is a mensch." In Judaism, this is one of the greatest compliments you can give someone. Marc met my father when he was a sophomore in high school and my father was about twenty-five. They first interacted with each other during a USY program, where Steve took Marc under his wing. He was almost like a mentor to Marc. Marc talked to me about those early years and mentioned how caring and good-natured Steve had always been with him. Although he loved to poke fun at Marc and never let him forget anything, the teasing always came from a good place. They started to grow close. My father had a crush on my mother at the time and wanted Marc's help with getting Lisa to notice him—and he was extremely persistent in this. He insisted that Marc had to convince his sister to go on a date with him; he would not give up. And of course, Marc eventually did convince Lisa to date Steve. The rest, as they say, is history.

During his college years, Marc lived with Steve for one semester, as part of a work-study co-op program. My parents were already dating by that point. That is when Marc got to know Steven better. He saw that Steve would do whatever it took to help his family and friends. Steve would soon become one of the first people Marc went to for advice and help.

Marc says that the best advice he ever got from Steve was this: "When you're having a bad day or even a couple of bad days, and nothing is going right, treat tomorrow as another day. Think of life like a sine-wave curve; it goes up and down. Everyone has good and bad days."

Nearly twenty years have passed since my father passed away. Still, I try to follow the very same advice Steve shared with Marc on that day and to live by the same principles he had instilled in me as a kid. I still remember him telling me: *"Josh, there are many growing pains on the way to the top. Acknowledging those pains and reflecting on them will give you the strength to keep climbing that mountain."* A sort of equation began to emerge in my mind: pain + reflection = progress. There are many hurdles in life; it's just a matter of how you react to them. Learning how to adapt and pivot in order to overcome those hurdles will make you a stronger person. Much like a chameleon changes colors to adapt to its environment, we humans change. We adapt. We learn.

This advice would also prove extremely helpful for Marc later on, when my father got sick. No matter how cancer affects your life – whether it touches you or someone you love – it will always challenge and change you. Everyone's got a different response to it. There are different things we home in on, different things that stay with us. For Marc, my father's illness drove home two important lessons. The first, perhaps, sounds commonplace, though it is no less true and powerful for that: Steve's death was a reminder of how brief and fragile life is. Marc was the only person besides my mother who was there at the hospital the day my father passed away. That was when it all became real for him. Watching someone you love die is one of the toughest things you can endure—and Steve had been the closest thing to a brother Marc had ever had, a person who had had a monumental impact on him. So it is only to be expected that his death tested him; it proved just how delicate life was.

The second is something Marc talked about a lot after my father's passing and that has stayed with me through the years. Marc shared with me that, even during the very worst times, when Steve was on his last legs, he never stopped smiling. Throughout the many chemotherapy sessions, several surgeries, and all of the time spent in rehabilitation, he always kept his cheerful demeanor and never stopped trying to make people laugh. Even in the final months of his life, he never let on that he was in pain and struggling. He tried to smile through it all.

This can also be seen in my father's writing. As I flipped through the pages of this journal, expecting to find that moment when Steve's optimism would fade and he would realize that his disease might prove fatal, I was surprised to see that this moment never came. Steve's underlying attitude stayed cool, calm, and collected throughout the entire duration of his illness. He always had this feisty attitude, as if he had something to prove. As if there was a chip on his shoulder. Regardless of what the doctors would tell him or what advice people would give him, he always tried to think outside the box, to search for alternative treatments, to look at the illness from a new perspective. He never gave up. This attitude has been very impactful in my life: it has taught me perseverance and has made me want to strive to better myself in any way I can. This is something I continue to work on every single day.

This is a life lesson that is not only useful to those whose lives have been touched by something as monumental as cancer or the death of a close family member. This dogged refusal to give up, this constant search for a new pathway to achieving your goals is applicable in any situation. Whether you feel you embody this trait or not, I challenge you to try thinking about your problem differently. If your mental and physical resources are too depleted to do it yourself, seek others who can provide a different point of view. Ask yourself the tough questions; your future self will thank you for it. Whether you get the answers you were looking for or not, you will achieve a deeper state of consciousness. This will help you identify exactly what you need to do to adapt your plan and find which benchmarks you need to change— while staying true to your life goal and to yourself.

After my father passed, I was given the honor of receiving an award on his behalf. This award was presented by the Jewish Home for the Aged in New Haven, Connecticut. Steve had served as their President of the Board of Directors for many years. The award was called *Keter Shem Tov*. It is given to those who demonstrate great leadership and community outreach skills in the local New Haven Jewish elderly community. The gratitude and respect I could sense among the people who filled the banquet halls had a very humbling effect on me. I saw what a lasting effect Steve had had on people, how involved and passionate he had been, to the very end.

This award ceremony was only a few months after my father's death. I was 10 years old at the time. As I entered my teenage years, I started to think differently about myself and about my father. Naturally, when you hit adolescence, you undergo a process of growth and change—not only in your body but also in your mind. I started asking questions about my father and realized I did not know much about who he had really been. As you can imagine, this can be troubling for someone that age. Without even realizing it, I started to question other things, things related to how I had been raised and the kind of person I was turning into. I began to think deeper about different aspects of life and examine parts of my personality I had not previously delved into. I was transforming from a boy into man, but what kind of man? I suddenly wanted to become a more well-rounded person, a contributor to society and not merely a spectator. In truth, I hoped that one day I may become, like my father before me, a *mensch*.

I wondered whether I would be able to accomplish that goal without my father around.

This brings us to my Bar Mitzvah. This is a significant day in Jewish religion, one in which we celebrate a child becoming a young man or woman. Typically, it happens at the age of thirteen for men and twelve for women. It is a great excuse for your family and friends to come together and watch you recite certain prayers or read from the Torah, or Old Testament. My Rabbi, Benjamin Scolnic of Temple Beth Shalom in Hamden, Connecticut, had known my father very well. He knew how important this day was to me and my family. He also knew how much it would have meant to Steve. In the days leading up to the big day, I can remember sitting in my Rabbi's office while he regaled me with a seemingly endless series of funny stories about my father. One important thing I discussed with my Rabbi that day is something that had also been on my father's mind following his diagnosis:

Steve Grove:

So now the question I ask myself at 37 is what to do with my life? What should I do now? What is next? And most importantly, what is the meaning of my life?

I know that my Rabbi, Benjamin Scolnic, is always preaching about helping others and doing for others; another Rabbi I know says that spirituality will drive me and show me the way; Rabbi Adam Kligfeld, a close friend of mine for many years (I knew him when he was just Adam), even gave me permission to be miserable, upset, and mad. How confusing is all of this?

Josh Grove:

After reading how important it was for my father to question his life's purpose, I knew, as I know now, that I had not been wrong in questioning mine. When I look back on my Bar Mitzvah now, I know my father was there in spirit. I cannot overstate the effect this day had on me and who I am today. To this day, I consider my Bar Mitzvah – the day I became a man according to the Jewish religion – to be the true starting point of my life. It was the day I embarked on the search for who my father really was, while at the same time I also started a journey of self-discovery. See, I was also trying to find out who *I* really was—and more importantly, who I can become. So I paused to reflect on this, and then charted a course for the future. How could I take the first step towards becoming who I wanted to become? The first goal I set myself was to find a way to reach out to the community of people affected by cancer.

Growing up, I had always wanted to get involved in *Relay for Life*. I had participated in one of their events as part of my Bar Mitzvah project. The *bar/bat* (*bar* for boys and *bat* for girls) project is an act of unselfishness that one must do before becoming a bar/bat mitzvah. It is quite a common practice and should consist of an action that exemplifies who that person wants to be in society. My project was completed prior to the big day. I chose to help raise money and awareness towards cancer research. It was a good starting point for me and an opportunity to get involved in an organization that I felt strongly about, while at the same time, it helped me to remember and reconnect with my father.

Right after college, I began to reach out to other people who had dealt with cancer in the past or who were still dealing with cancer. Whether it was through *Relay for Life*, or other cancer-related charities, I started to become more involved in this community; I started listening to others' stories. This made me more and more passionate about raising awareness and money for cancer. I tried to share my ideals with everyone and anyone I could. It became an addictive feeling. Sometimes I had to adapt and adjust, but I never deviated from what I now knew to be my life path: "Never change the goal; change the plan." Of course, my early experiences with my father's illness shaped me a lot in that regard. When I was younger, I used to dream about the day when all cancers would be curable. While this has not happened, cancer research has come a long way in recent years, and I do believe we are heading in the right direction. It is not a straightforward journey, of course. But one thing I learned from my father is that it is important to keep fighting, to never give up on your dreams.

And it is also important, as my father did in his journal, to stop and appreciate those who help you along the way, to celebrate the small victories. As you grow older, you gain new perspective and may start to see certain events in your life in a new light. I will never forget the first day I stepped into my Rabbi's office to practice, leading up to my Bar Mitzvah. He said, "You know, Josh, your father would be tremendously proud of you today." I was not sure how to react. My father had not even been gone five years, yet I had started to question statements like that because I had already realized I didn't really know my father that well. How could I know if what he was saying was true? My Rabbi went on to say how much Steve talked about me and how proud he was of my every milestone or accomplishment, no matter how big or small. Given my age at the time, I don't think I understood the true message behind what he was telling me. Nevertheless, as I grew older, the message started to sink in. What he was really saying was, while you look to the future, stop to take pleasure in the present. What he was really saying was, the little things matter; take the time to enjoy and celebrate them. What he was really saying was, while moving forward, don't forget to occasionally stand still and admire the view.

Chapter 6: The Little Things, Good and Bad

Josh Grove:

You might be tempted to think that, when you deal with a disease like cancer, every other worry in life falls by the wayside: jobs, chores, financial issues, family problems, great and small misfortunes, surely they will suddenly all seem unimportant. It's true that, to some degree, your life revolves around managing the disease; but the little stresses can also take their toll, making dealing with the disease itself even harder. This next excerpt gives you an idea of the impact these stresses had on my father:

Steve Grove:

I will tell you about the role stress has played in this terrible disease. In the past twelve months, from June 1999 to June 2000, our family experienced two failed pregnancies, we sold our home, lost our building lot for a new house, got another building lot, built a new house, moved into an apartment, dealt with our son staying back in first grade, lived in a small apartment all winter with most of our life in storage, had a van stolen, had another car die on us, bought two cars, moved into our new house, had massive employee and business problems, my wife lost her job, we settled on never having any more children naturally, started an adoption process to adopt in Russia and then adjusted to my wife finding a new job. If that doesn't make you tired, it should. Anyone who tells me that stress plays no part in cancer is wrong. And that's just in the past year. If we go back a few years, you'll see this is just the tip of the iceberg. Thankfully, we've still had good moments along the way. I am not sure when we will manage to catch our breath from this new bump in the road, but I hope it is soon.

Josh Grove:

Times of crisis test us, but they also show us what is truly important: your loved ones and your health, the little joys in life. In times of need, your friends and family provide a sense of comfort that cannot be felt any other way. Spending time with the people you love, laughing, sharing stories, and being there for each other minimizes your reaction to stress and makes everyday problems suddenly seem solvable. Whether you're spending time with them in the hospital or at home, everyone knows the reason you are all there, which makes the time spent together that much more special. I can attest to this from my own experience. It is as if the obstacles we are faced with shed light on the things and people that matter in our lives; they bring an awareness that cannot be gleaned otherwise. This also makes clear which things do not matter and should be let go. Differentiating between the two, helping people to realize what is important and what is not, is what Steve saw as one of the goals of the book:

Steve Grove:

The stress that we deal with in life has got to affect us. We don't eat right, don't sleep right, and make a big issue out of trifles. Many people in my life have complained at length about issues that just don't matter. I understand that people have their own lives and problems, but many fail to see that life is larger than where they are at any point in time. How do you get someone to realize that it's time to relax, and stop being so concerned with unimportant things? I laugh now when I think about the various customers I have had through the years who have left me because their work didn't get done fast enough. They had an issue that needed fixing, they wanted you to give it your full attention, and that was that. I used to think that most customers are only happy if you are strapped to your desk 24 hours a day, 7 days a week. Sometimes, stress has caused death through alcoholism, disease, or even suicide. What can be so important that we can't be patient with each other?

Have you ever stood in line at a store? There is nothing that you can do other than stand in line. And the same goes for sitting in traffic. What is the purpose of getting agitated and stressed when there is nothing you can do about it? As I started to write this book, it became so evident to me: we live our lives in the craziest of fashions. What has our society turned into?

Perhaps those of us who are sick are here to remind the rest of the world to slow down. I'll be fine, and I'll get better, but somehow I feel I will be a changed person. Sitting and watching TV with my son and wife seems like such a small thing, yet it is so meaningful and enjoyable. It means so much more than any Broadway show or dinner out. We must all learn to recognize and appreciate the small moments in life, and this book will hopefully remind you to do just that. Enough is enough, people! Society needs to get a grip and realize what is truly important.

Without your health, there is nothing to be happy about. Oh, there are joys along the way, and you will forget your problems at times, but to enjoy life, you need health, family, and friends. Amazingly, those things cost nothing.

Josh Grove:

Now that you have heard a bit about Steve's upbringing from my uncle, you know that he was a man who struggled not just with cancer, but also with his identity. Add to this the various other stresses my father mentions here, and you can tell it can't have been easy for him; yet he shifts his focus on the positive and manages to find moments of happiness even in the midst of hardship. Remember that, while you may be struggling inside, it is okay to use life as a distraction; it is okay to take joy and comfort in your loved ones. Being diagnosed with cancer is not something I can personally relate to, of course; what I know is only how it affected both me and my family. But I do think that my father had the right idea about the things that really matter: friends, family, health. I have mentioned before that writing his book was also, in a way, a search for my father, for the person he was—I have been unconsciously seeking things we may have had in common. In reading the above paragraphs, I thought, perhaps I do look at life in the same way as my father.

Steve Grove:

I had major surgery that I had to recover from for a month before I could move ahead to the next stage. There was a recuperation period and I was feeling lousy from surgery and lousy when thinking about the next stage. Of course, not being at work and giving up a paycheck for several months didn't help. I often wondered, in fact, if I could actually feel any lousier. But then I told myself, "I guess it can always get worse."

Now, let us review that statement: it can always get worse. This is one of the things that helped me take everything that was happening to me in stride. I tried to review where I was according to the rest of the world and remain grateful for small comforts. You may not want to be thankful for indoor plumbing and air conditioning, but when you think about it, the majority of the world does not have running water or flush toilets, so we ought to be thankful for that.

Josh Grove:

Developing gratitude for the little things in life has been instrumental to my growth as a person. And it has especially helped me when it comes to overcoming obstacles. It is so easy to succumb to the frenetic rhythms of modern life and dwell on unimportant things, rather than staying grounded in the present moment. In this aspect, I take a great deal of pride in continuously working on myself. No matter how hard things get, I try to remember to be grateful for what is going well in my life, just like my father, who never took anything or anyone for granted.

In his journal, Steve often talks about the little things that helped him cope with his illness. He reflects on the quiet moments and funny anecdotes that brightened his days and made his suffering more bearable. He loved hearing a good joke and absolutely loved telling stories. I hope that his friends and family will want to share his stories with others well into the future. But I hope you also share your own. I hope you take the time to identify what makes you happy. How is it that you cope with stress? What has helped you before when you have gone through a difficult time? What are the small things you can be grateful for today? Try to stay in a forward-thinking mindset: e.g., ask yourself, "In the future, how can I incorporate more of the things that give me joy into my life?" Focus on what is truly important to you. The things that give you joy can be physical, intellectual, or spiritual pleasures—keeping both your mind at peace and your body in balance is key, especially when the daily stresses of life pile up.

Another thing that can help you cope with stress – it certainly helped my father – was humor. If you ask anyone who knew Steve, they will tell you that his sense of humor was quite dry. He was quick-witted, too; his mind was always spinning at a hundred miles an hour. Often, you had to peel back several layers to understand the humor in his jokes. Providing comedic relief and "lightening the mood" was something that came easily to him and something he incorporated into his life, both in his early years and while he battled cancer. It was his way of relating with people, of feeling connected.

Steve Grove:

When I realized that I was sicker than just a mild case of diverticulitis, as was previously thought in late June 2000, I started to write. I tried to talk about the things that happened to me, and focused on the lighter side of many of them. I started to notice the things that made me laugh. Many people encouraged me to carry around a pad and write down the things that struck me as funny. I have been home from the hospital for months and have had plenty of time to convert my notes and thoughts into a book. I am hoping that I will have people help me edit and make corrections later, but for now, I am just writing. It helps.

Josh Grove:

Many of his close friends would talk to me about Steve's sense of humor, years after he had passed. They would share memories of it in action—comments, jokes, anecdotes. It was his fun-loving personality, above all, that they remembered most; there was no situation, no matter how stressful or grim, in which he could not find something to laugh about. One of his friends, Dena Shulman, told me: "Steve was one of those people who could find humor in anything. He liked seeing people smile." There is so much meaning behind that, but it took me a long time to truly understand it. A smile, in his mind, symbolized a moment in which someone forgot about their hardships and difficulties, if only for a second. He knew that even that one second was important and, for each person, it could make the difference between coping with life's stresses or sinking under the weight of their burdens.

As I got older, I started to understand how important humor was in my own life—how the ability to laugh in a difficult situation has helped not just me, but those around me. Surrounding yourself with people who laugh as much as you is a sure-fire way to boost your own mood, energy, and psychological resilience. I started to realize that it was important to me to make sure people around me are laughing, smiling, and enjoying themselves, even if it is at my expense. After all, we should all be able to laugh at ourselves!

People who have known me for a long time now know that I try not to take life too seriously. At the end of the day, laughing is one of the healthiest things you can do for yourself. One of my heroes growing up, Jim Valvano, said, as he was receiving his ESPYs Arthur Ashe Courage Award for his battle with cancer: "If you laugh, think, and cry, that's a full day. That's a heck of a day. You do that seven days a week, you're going to have something special." I've tried to keep that in mind through every phase of my life.

Steve Grove:

The book documents my life from June 24, 2000 onward. I am not going to try to give an account of my whole life before that in these pages. But maybe if this goes well, I will go back and chronicle what has been a life of ups and downs. I have spoken with some people in my office about getting an author to write about how I have possibly made it through all the adversity that I have faced in my short 37 years here. I am amazed at times at what I have been able to endure in terms of problems and often think about getting more books written. We'll have to see how this book does.

I do want to apologize, however, to the EMBA program at the University of New Haven for writing this book before finishing my MBA thesis. The thesis is done, but I still have to submit a final draft to my advisor in order to get my degree. I completed my coursework in December 1999 and have not had a chance to finish my draft. I know that, if this book is published, they'll wonder when I plan on finishing my thesis. I promise that the next writing I will do will be my thesis!

Josh Grove:

Reading through the pages of his journal, it struck me that my father took the time to explain how he felt in each given moment as he underwent this difficult journey; he gave a detailed account of the medical process, while not skipping over the anecdotes and light moments; he took pains to document what happened at each juncture of this battle with cancer. And he did this at a time when he may have been in physical pain, or struggling emotionally. I then realized I had found another facet of my father's personality that I could relate to: his work ethic.

One of Steve's oldest friends, Chris Nowacki, talked to me about how his memories of Steve in college: "He was a well-put-together person, mature beyond his years. You would not have thought that about him. He was organized, an extremely good leader, enthusiastic, and a go-getter type of person." Many others shared with me that, no matter what challenge Steve took on, if he was involved, you never had to worry: you would always be in good hands with Steve. He felt that working hard and being involved in various projects and organizations outside of school would help him grow; it would give him the foundational skills to develop as a man. It's clear from the effort he put into this new challenge he had set himself – putting pen to paper every day and diligently documenting his illness – that, to my father, work was another of the many little things that gave life meaning, that could help to relieve life's stresses. I believe that writing this book gave my father purpose. He threw himself into it with admirable dedication, and it became his goal to share it with the world and help others.

I had known as a child that my father really enjoyed being a multi-tasker; I remember that he was always involved in multiple things at once. And after his passing, several of my father's friends were kind enough to share with me some of their memories of when Steve was twenty-one and a college student at Quinnipiac University in Hamden, Connecticut. It took my father almost seven years to complete his accounting degree. At first, his parents helped him pay for college. He had also earned several scholarships to help cover the costs. But, early on, Steve contracted Hepatitis C and had to drop out for a semester or two. He was also living through a rocky situation at home. He ultimately lost his scholarships and could not continue to help pay for school, thus attending only part-time while working multiple jobs. Hearing that Steve had not finished his MBA before he passed was not surprising to me. Steve had to edit his thesis and resubmit it, but he kept procrastinating. When he was diagnosed with colon cancer, this project was put on the back burner. He was eventually awarded his MBA from the University of New Haven posthumously.

As Steve strived to help others, I urge you to do your part. You probably have certain goals for tomorrow, next year, or ten years from now. Maybe you even have a plan and concrete actions mapped out for achieving them. As you create the path you want to take, and follow that path, you will start to feel the results of your actions. But each action should stem from a larger goal—what do you want to accomplish by doing this? How will it help you and others? It is the bigger-picture goals that this book is urging you to strive for—the ones that affect others, too, whether they are close friends or people far from your circle. Think of how you can make a positive impact in someone else's life, just as Steve intended to with this book. And remember that throwing yourself into a task, giving it your full effort, as my father did with his writing, can also help you, as well as others.

There is a crucial difference to be made here, and that brings me back to the issue of stress. Steve was always taking on more than he should, which meant that his workload continued to grow until it got to the point of overload. In some ways, he was adding more and more stress to his life with each new project he undertook. But some of this was positive stress. Writing a book in the midst of cancer treatments is, in a way, adding extra stress to a stressful situation, but for Steve it was also the remedy to other, negative stresses he was dealing with. It's important to mention that stress can also be a good thing: it can be an impetus for action and change. Think about what stress means to you. As you deal with the daily obstacles we all face, try to keep in the back of your mind the difference between good and bad stressors. Good stress can help you deal with problems, as it helped my father. Bad stress only worsens them; it affects not only you, but also the people around you.

As you get older, you start to separate the unnecessary stresses from the necessary ones. You are able to categorize problems into levels of importance and can prioritize them, so that they are not harmful or detrimental to your body and mind. It has been a life-long goal of mine to show people how controlling stressors can drastically enhance their lives. Becoming comfortable with good stress is key here. You must learn to live with some degree of discomfort, as this discomfort is necessary in order to grow. My father believed, as do I, that if you try and live your life completely stress-free, you are not fully living. Stress is a part of life. Do not avoid it entirely, because ultimately feelings of stagnation and contention set in. Instead, try to operate uncomfortably. It will help make you stronger and in turn allow you to help those around you as well. Gaining the ability to differentiate between good and bad stressors, as well as learning to pursue and use good stressors in a positive way, is crucial in achieving the goals you set for yourself.

Finally, there is one more trick my father had up his sleeve, one more "little thing" that helped him face an uncertain future. This is a simple – but difficult to accomplish – mental adjustment that you can make to cope with life's stresses: remaining hopeful and forward-thinking.

Steve Grove:

I look forward to sitting around Oprah, The View, Jerry Springer, Queen Latifah, and Rosie (I've watched a lot of daytime TV while recuperating) and laughing about all that went on. I hope that many parts in this book will make you laugh out loud. Some of it you won't even believe, but trust me: I am not making any of this up. The truth is almost always funnier than anything you could make up.

Josh Grove:

I have read that again and again: "I look forward to laughing about all that went on." Giving up was never an option for my father. Staying forward-oriented was his way of dealing with the stress he was under. He believed that he saw his battle with cancer as just another chapter in his life, while his victory in this battle would be another notch in his belt. The man was struggling tremendously, and yet continued to have an optimistic outlook on life, to put a positive spin on things. He was looking at an uncertain, thorny path ahead and yet kept going.

It is this mentality where perhaps I resemble my father most. Opening your mind up to cancer and getting involved in the battle against it is not an easy thing to pick up as a hobby. My goal of having even the smallest impact on the cancer community was one that I was determined not to give up on—and this book is a direct outcome of that doggedness. In the same way, Steve's determination to beat cancer and tell his story as a survivor is something that crops up again and again in his journal. These two goals were constantly on my father's mind and became somewhat interrelated: he would survive to get to tell the story. This tenacity shows me who my father really was. So here is Steve, dreaming of a future he would never get to have, in his typical dry sense of humor:

Steve Grove:

The ultimate question about the book is, of course, who will play me in the movie version! I know you are laughing at this point, as we don't even know if we will be published, but it's fun to think about that...

Chapter 7: Controlling the Controllable

Steve Grove:

Finding out that you have cancer is one of those moments. What do you do first, second, or third? There is a rush of thoughts that go through your head, and you just don't know which impulse to act on first. You just feel lost. It is almost like you wish someone will wake you up from the nightmare so you can go on with all the nonsense that you had filled your life with before. You are looking down the road at a long and exhausting trail and you're wondering when it will end...

Josh Grove:

Imagine you are suddenly diagnosed with cancer. Or perhaps you don't need to go that far: imagine you are faced with an unexpected problem, something that throws you for a loop. There is nothing that can prepare you for it. First, you feel lost and unsure what to do. How do you react? What actions do you take? What do you prioritize? It can be hard to formulate an overarching goal, let alone determine the actions needed to achieve it. This first step can be the most difficult. It can be daunting to look at the road ahead and find no concrete steps to follow, no map to guide you.

But then you start to break it down into smaller steps. Pivoting your mindset into ignition is key. This is the point where your fight-or-flight response kicks in, which can be the critical point in your process. Growing up, I was someone who always chose to fight. And I realized as I read this journal that this might be something I have gotten from my father.

Steve knew that he was facing an uphill battle. He knew he would have to first get all the pieces of the puzzle, and then assemble them in the correct order. He soon realized that, by remaining forward-thinking and focusing on one action at a time, he could accomplish them one by one. Slowly but surely, he would be able to check off the tasks he needed to accomplish on his way to reaching his goal, which was to beat cancer. He also knew there were things over which he had no control. So he decided to focus on controlling the controllable.

Steve Grove:

You will feel emotional. There is nothing wrong with that feeling, but you need to get over it. You need to determine where to start and how to face the new reality that you were just informed of. The faster you are able to really understand that life is 1/3 attitude, 1/3 luck, and 1/3 everything else, the better off you will be, and again your future self will thank you. You can control 2/3 and do a lot of praying to help in the luck department.

Josh Grove:

Many of the goals I set myself first started as a lengthy list of daunting tasks that got shorter over time; progress doesn't happen all at once. I would set a goal, break it down into achievable benchmarks, and tackle each benchmark at a time. I knew that by staying hungry and focusing on getting better, I would accomplish my goal. Perhaps the best thing you can do when you stumble upon (what seems like) an insurmountable issue is to get up and go about your day as you would at any other time; this will keep your mind at peace. At the same time, try to break down the problem into smaller tasks that can be accomplished, and stay focused on the task at hand. That way, you will not feel overwhelmed by the enormity of the problem.

Having a focus will not only simplify your life but will help you develop a forward-thinking mindset and allow you to zero in on the things that matter. We can spend our lives getting mired in chores and work, accumulating wealth and possessions, and going around in circles with no concrete goal or purpose in mind. This is not to say work and money cannot be part of your goals; if they are important to you, there is absolutely nothing wrong with that. Just make sure your goal is one you have actually set for yourself and not simply something you are pursuing because everyone else is. Ask yourself: why do I want to accomplish this? Why this goal, and not the other? Why is this important to me? In other words, find your "Why?" and move on from there. And remember that part of staying goal-focused is focusing on what you can control and leaving the rest up to chance and fate.

So what can you control? In my personal life, when I am faced with a task, whether easy or tough, my first step is to acquire as much knowledge about it as possible, then come up with a rough plan.

Growing up, I always felt that staying curious and having a questioning mindset would become a very important skill later in life, and it has helped me enormously in the first stages of goal-setting. I cannot describe the sense of kinship and recognition I felt when I read these passages and saw that my father felt the same way. It's clear that the first step Steve took is to seek information about his illness. Having cancer does not come with directions, so he tried to arm himself with as much knowledge as possible. After all, in order to devise a plan, you must first have all the facts.

Steve Grove:

Information will offer you hope and lack of hope. Information will also offer you faith and the lack of faith. We have entered such an information age that you can find out everything there is to know about your condition, what other people experience, and how it does or doesn't affect others. You can also get yourself statistic after statistic on website after website. I suggest you look at some of them and rely upon your local physicians to fill in the blanks. (…) I tried to contact the American Cancer Society before I went in for surgery. Perhaps you'll do better with them than I did. I wanted some information, left messages, and called a few times. I suggest you do the same.

Josh Grove:

Sometimes Steve felt there was too much information available, or that it was contradictory or repetitive. Again, this first stage can be overwhelming, but it is important to gather all the information you can, then sort through it and take what you need.

Steve Grove:

The amount of information you will receive will be enough to make you crazy. I hit thirty-two websites when I entered "colon cancer" on Yahoo. It would have taken me weeks to read all the information available. I took some of it and left some of it behind. Wait until you get into the hospital and all those information volunteers come and see you. They are all well-meaning, and you'll need another suitcase to take home all the books, brochures, pamphlets, and flyers they will leave you. Trust me, you will be overwhelmed with information. Some of it will be helpful and some will just repeat the same things time and time again. I only needed to know once that red meats are something I should avoid. I was never really much of a red meat eater anyhow, so I didn't need eighteen brochures about it.

Josh Grove:

Technology has really developed since my father originally wrote this book, 20-plus years ago. The internet was not as big of a thing as it is now. Social media was not a thing. A browser search then turned up 32 results for colon cancer; a similar search now will turn up over 500 million results—a veritable deluge of information, and not all of it accurate. It can be difficult to separate professional medical websites from advertising, irrelevant information, pseudoscience, or misinformation. Even then, Steve knew that the information that was being shared with him may or may not have been applicable to him. But he also knew that gathering many different opinions was important.

If there is one thing I have learned over the years is to listen to everything that is thrown at you. Do not dismiss any opinion; absorb as many facts and perspectives as you can, and file them in the back of your mind. That is not to say that you should not be discerning. You do not necessarily have to listen to every piece of advice you are given, but simply have it available at your fingertips. You never know what might be helpful to you down the road. Always remember that knowledge is power. Doing your own research and forming your own opinion is important; however, being able to sit on the other side of the table can provide you with a different perspective. You may reframe the problem or see it from a different lens that you may not have seen or heard before.

My father had a similar mentality. After exhausting the reading materials provided to him, he turned to other people for counsel. He sought out advice from those who had faced the same battle.

Steve Grove:

It helps to talk to others who have been through similar experiences. I can tell you that a few conversations I have had with people who have been through what I am going through were truly helpful. You really can't imagine the various issues unless you are going through them. Everyone will try to give you advice and will try to understand, but talking to others who have been through this will help.

There are tons of books out there that people will tell you to read, and they will even buy them for you. Articles and brochures will begin to come out of your ears. At times, you will not want to read, and many books just aren't for you. There is nothing wrong with you if some of the books are not for you, and you just leave them on the bookshelf to gather dust. I guess I hope you only choose to read this book for yourself... This is a good one not to miss!

As for talking to your family and children, everyone deals with this differently. It is easier for all of you if you can be strong and show your children that they don't have to worry. I feel strongly that you should be open and honest about your situation, and I think that this extends to your own children. This will help them mature. There are some good books out there that your children can read, or that you can read to them. This type of discussion and understanding will help your children to see this for what it is: a disease that people fight and get better from, like and unlike many others. Share with them your issues and let them feel with you some of the ups and downs, but don't dwell on the disease; try to maintain as normal a life as you possibly can. You first have to determine what normal is. What family with children can point to a normal day anyhow?

Josh Grove:

Each problem is different. No two situations are the same, and even two people faced with the same situation may respond to it in a completely different manner. Sometimes, when you are dealing with an issue, you may have contradictory advice bestowed upon you. I went through the same thing after my father's passing. It was tough having to swallow the fact that my father died of cancer; it took a long time for me to fully come to terms with it. It felt unfair I had been dealt the cards that I was dealt, so I tried to talk to many different people, to look at my struggle from different points of view. I found that everyone wanted to give me advice, and not one opinion agreed with those that had come before it. Ultimately, I had to choose the advice that was helpful and then process it on my own.

My father, too, found that everyone had an opinion on his diagnosis, treatment, plan of action, emotional wellbeing, etc. Everyone wanted to help. But at the end of the day, he knew that it was up to him to call the shots and make his own decisions. If you are in a situation in which you have to make similarly difficult decisions, my only advice is to be patient and take the time to take it all in. Whatever you come up with will be your own unique solution. At the end of the day, you can only weigh all options available, make a decision, and try to stay calm and focused on your goal. With your goal in mind, you will formulate a plan of action based on the information available to you, either from experts, books, or others who have overcome the same problem.

Of course, sometimes you find out that the information is one thing, and the reality is quite another. What do you do then? My father found that nothing can fully prepare you for going through chemotherapy. Each person's experience is different.

Steve Grove:

You'll be on medications that may not work and that may take days to kick in. I had spasms that started four days after I came home from surgery and lasted for one whole week. It took the doctors four days to get the medication right, and then my muscles ached for almost two weeks after the spasms stopped. There is nothing written in any book about when you'll feel better and what complications you will and will not experience. Take the medications and let them make you feel better. Then, when you are feeling better on your own, stop the medicines. Life is much easier without any drugs. You will agree with me if you ever experience this. The drugs that they use these days are short-acting and non-habit-forming, but their side effects can often be worse than the disease they are treating.

Josh Grove:

Learning new things – either from others or from experience – can lead to introducing additional steps as part of your plan. These steps will continue to multiply as you progress towards your goal. Yet the goal stays the same. No matter how much you prepare in advance and how many of your benchmarks you achieve, changes along the way are necessary. You always have to adjust your plan, your coping strategies, your expectations. Be prepared for this, and remember that the path to reaching your goal is never a straight line.

Steve Grove:

Your emotions are going to be up and down. You'll become hopeful at times and hopeless at others. Some days you'll feel like you can run a four-minute mile; some days you'll feel lousy and just eating breakfast will be a big effort. You don't know what will set you off, either. You will have many days when you feel negative and upset. But the more time goes by, the more your treatments are successful, and the better you feel, the more you will be able to keep a positive outlook on things.

I know this sounds corny, but your purpose will drive you. Remember to keep moving forwards. Always seek that motivation in you to do more and do it for yourself. I wanted to recuperate from the surgery, so I worked at it. I ate a little more each day and moved about more, also. As I moved about, I felt stronger, and each day I was able to do more. You're going to have setbacks, and there are going to be days that you don't feel like doing much, but resist the temptation to give up. Think of those days as just bumps in the road and attempt to move ahead in the best way that you know how.

Josh Grove:

Even when you set yourself attainable goals, there will always be ups and downs. Battling cancer is a long road, and on some days the path to recovery may seem longer and more difficult than others. At times, your willpower will falter. At times, you will feel tired or emotional. This is normal, but it's important to not get distracted by the stumbling blocks along the road. Keep an eye on the path ahead and keep adapting your plan, while always keeping the goal in sight. Having the right support system will be extremely beneficial in this; your closest people can help you keep perspective on days when the obstacles feel impossible to overcome. Seeing the bigger picture may be tough in the moment, but you must stay focused on the goal and keep hacking away at it. This is something that I have learned from my father and something that I try to work on every day. Remember: setbacks are normal; fighting to overcome them or giving up is what makes all the difference.

Steve Grove:

You will get advice. Oh boy, will you get advice! Every single person will have so many things to tell you about what to do, what to expect, how horrible certain things are, or what you will go through. Don't listen to anyone. You really have to understand that each and every case and person are different. There may be similarities between you and your case, but chances are, things will be different from what others will tell you.

Josh Grove:

As we turn the corner in the story keep this in mind: your health is the single most important thing there is. When you have to make decisions on it, and are given more information and advice than you know what to do with, the best thing you can do for yourself is to take it all in. Let it sink in and see what sticks. Talk to your friends and family. Let them give their opinions. Then, form your own opinion. Own it. Stay true to yourself. Ultimately, no matter how selfish it may feel, you must make your own educated decision on what is best for you and only you.

Chapter 8: Hope & Faith

Steve Grove:

It is important to stay positive and keep faith and hope in every step you take. Those two words become your daily goal. You must look to your physicians and nurses to help you understand where your hope should be placed, but the key is to find hope and faith somewhere. This is not to say that you will not feel sad or upset. And it is not to say that you should not *feel sad and upset. You will. On some days, the hardest thing you are going to do will be to get up, get showered, get dressed, and move on. You'll feel despair, wonder, and even depression at times, but you have to work with them. There is nothing wrong with these and all your feelings.*

I have read enough books, magazines, pamphlets, articles, notes, and letters to choke me. People have sent me every type of reading material you can think of on being positive, having hope, and not losing faith. Your religious leaders will encourage you, and the world will push you to keep moving forward.

Josh Grove:

I talked in the previous chapter about staying goal-focused and forward-thinking. You must look at the situation and see what you can and cannot control, and focus on the former, even if that means having to take two steps back to go one step forward. And for each step you take, always remember your *why*: the reasons why you get up in the morning, why you go to work every day, why you fight. Your *why* is your purpose, and this will help you stay driven and focused on those things you can control. But what about the things you cannot control? Those are best left up to chance and the higher beings. Staying committed and knowing that you are doing what you can to control the controllable can make the hoping and praying part easier.

Steve Grove:

I have always been big in the hope and faith area. I suppose because I have had such a hard life the past 37 years, it's one of the few things I could escape into. Despite the problems and hardships I encountered, I trained myself to keep calm and look on the bright side of things. Being able to look at the glass half full will set you apart from the rest. Having a positive attitude will push out all the negative thoughts and feelings. You must train yourself to feel hopeful and look forward to the end of the problem. You'll have to do this for yourself. There is help, and there are people out there to give you hope, but you'll have to find it inside yourself first.

You will be alone frequently, and you may need to dig down quite deep to find that hope for the future. Get your facts clear and then hold on to the positive ones. It will not be easy, and you will be down at times, but that's normal. Let it pass and then move on. Keeping busy and having a purpose will help.

Josh Grove:

Digging deep inside yourself to find the hope and drive to keep going is hard; it is an aspect of my own life where I have had to make tremendous effort. As you continue to learn more about yourself, push yourself just that little bit more each day. Knowing that you can always get better can help you stay motivated. You can achieve anything you set your mind to, but for that you need to *believe* you can achieve it. It is much easier said than done, but Steve did it. He kept his hope and faith. At the end of the day, he believed he could get through it.

Steve Grove:

I was sick and had my surgery in September 2000. One of the rabbis I spoke to claimed that I had timed things perfectly to avoid having to be in synagogue for the marathon sessions that are held during the high holiday period of the Jewish New Year. I reminded the Rabbi that I didn't have to be in a synagogue to pray or to be spiritual. Many of the clergy will tell you that once you are better you can resume your attendance. But in the meantime, remember that no faith is determined by the walls of any religious institution. Your prayer and faith need to be a part of you. I am sure these prayers will be heard, and that's the true measurement of faith and religion. I hope I was able to teach the Rabbi something on that day.

Josh Grove:

Forgiveness is a basic tenet of many religions, something that is considered, for many, part and parcel of being a good person. The

Christian Bible counsels, "Forgive, and you will be forgiven." The Quran mentions that "whoever forgives and amends, he shall have his reward." My own religion, Judaism, reminds us that forgiveness benefits the forgiver as well as the forgiven: "I erase your transgressions for my sake, and your sins I will not remember." Forgiving those who have wronged us is something that many people have struggled with, and my father was no exception. But something as life-altering as cancer can give you a different perspective. Old grudges that may have once felt unpardonable may suddenly seem meaningless. Steve, too, found that he needed to forgive those who had wronged him and let old friends back into his life.

One thing that changed my father's opinion of people was when they started to appear in his hour of need. Whether they were faking an interest in his struggles or not, he tried to be polite and forgiving to those who had ignored him and pushed him away for many years. He always wondered why certain people popped in and out of his life on a regular basis and others he never heard a peep from. But in the last few years of his life, he wanted to give people a second chance and tried to view them in a different light. He felt it was the right thing to do, both morally and spiritually.

Steve Grove:

Forgiving will also help you heal. You'll soon realize how meaningless all of our daily anger and grudges truly are. Releasing any hardened feelings in your heart will make space for good feelings and a better attitude. I am not a psychiatrist, nor have I ever studied this in school. I just know human behavior and I know how forgiveness works. "I forgive you." Try to say it a few times and then listen to yourself. Tell yourself and convince yourself and others that you forgive them. Release those angry feelings and attempt to reconcile all those old frustrations. When it comes down to it, having your loved ones by your side is tremendously healing. So why not allow a few more friends or family back in? I know it sounds corny, but you'll be amazed at how good you will feel after doing it.

Josh Grove:

Eventually, my father turned to the big question that many religions have tried to solve: why? Why did this disease befall him? Why do bad things happen to certain people and not others? There are no easy answers, but Steve tried his best to grapple with this question and wrest meaning out of the struggle and hardship he had to undergo. I believe he did find a sort of answer, though it may not have been the one he expected.

Steve Grove:

You are going to spend some time asking yourself "Why?" I often pondered that in silence. It's not a question that people are going to be comfortable with. You are going to wonder why the arrow hits in one place and misses in other places. It's a question we had asked ourselves when we had to give up on having any more children naturally due to infertility. You see so many families mistreating and abusing their children, and you ask why. You see many families with far more children than they can handle, and you ask the same question.

When you get sick, it's the same thing. You want to know what you did wrong. Why did this happen to you? Why can't it be someone else? And there just isn't any answer. The answer is: "Just because." Asking "Why me?" is often a waste of time and emotions. It's natural to go through this, to wonder about these things, but then you have to move on. There is a great book called "When Bad Things Happen to Good People." It's by a Rabbi who had a son who died of a rare aging illness. This Rabbi goes on to tell people some very simple things, and the most important thing of all is that there is no answer to that question. You just have to have faith and hope that things will work out, and you have to appreciate life and live it well. That seems to be the only answer to the question "Why?"

There will also be good things that come from your illness. I know that I have seen my son leave for school every day for a month while I was at home recuperating. I know that I have had dinner with my family every evening for a month, and I feel like I have truly rested. I have met and reconnected with people I never thought I would see again. I have learned more about the importance of love, friends, and family than I could have from any client meeting or community event. I have had time to write this book, which will hopefully help others.

Maybe the question to ask isn't "Why do bad things happen to good people?" The real question is "How can the bad things that happen to good people help them become better people?"

Josh Grove:

Stop and take a few moments to let that one sink in. Many people have described my father as a good man, a person who treated others with respect. Why did he have to get sick, and not someone else? Was it just bad luck? Steve wrestled with this question in such a unique way.

As many others who have been touched by a grave illness, he started wondering if he was a good person. He wondered if he was a good enough husband, father, and friend. And then he decided to use this setback to become a better person; he believed the bad things that befall us can help us grow and become better people. There is no real answer as to why bad things happen to good people. But there is a lesson that can be drawn here: while there will always be highs and lows in life, it's how you respond to them that will shape who you are.

Steve and Josh (as a toddler)

**Steve and Josh at a family friends Bat Mitzvah
(Marla Spivack) in 2001**

Steve, Lisa, Josh, and employees
Opening of S. Grove & Associates in the '90s

Steve helping at a local minor league baseball outing sponsored by S. Grove & Associates called the New Haven Ravens

(Toronto Blue Jays Single A Team at the time)

Steve, Lisa, Josh, and his friend at the New Haven Ravens game

(Where Josh and his friend threw out the first pitch)

S. Grove & Associates was a major sponsor for the organization

S. Grove & Associates Office
Accounting Firm located in Hamden, Connecticut

Steve receiving an award from the Small Business Administration for his involvement in the community with S. Grove & Associates

Article recognizing Steve for work accomplishments in the
community

The Hamden Journal (A Local newspaper in Connecticut)
An article recognizing Steve in the community

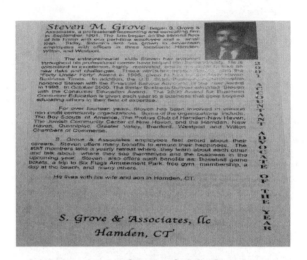

Article about Steve & his business

Magazine article written by Steve about financial planning advice

THIS WEEK IN BUSINESS

Grove firm wins small business award

Steven M. Grove of S. Grove & Associates has been named Accountant Advocate of the Year in Connecticut by the U.S. Small Business Administration.

The award is given to accountants who have contributed to providing a better economic and financial climate for small companies.

S. Grove & Associates is a midsize accounting and consulting firm offering services in business, accounting and consulting. This includes bookkeeping functions, financial management and consulting, business computer services and tax planning preparation.

S. Grove & Associate's main office is in Hamden, with other offices in Wilton and Westport.

The U.S. Small Business Administration, established in 1953, provides financial, technical and management assistance to help Americans start, run and expand their business.

The SBA is the nation's largest single financial backer of small businesses, and offered management and technical assistance last year to more than a million small business owners.

STEPHEN GROVE

Article about S. Grove & Associates winning small business award

David Gordon (Josh's godfather), Steve, and Lisa at David's
Wedding

Camp Sequassen Staff Picture 1986

(Steve pictured second row from bottom, five in from the right)

Steve teaching other staff about leadership

Steve and a troop he was leading at a local event in Connecticut

Camp Sequassen Staff Picture 1987
(Steve pictured second row from bottom, first one on the right)

Vice President of Camping & Camp Directors (two different years) Arrowheads (from the dining hall at Camp Sequassen where Steve spent many summers)

Steve Grove in Boy Scouts Uniform (early years)

Josh, Lisa, and Steve at Lisa's brother, Marc's wedding

Josh and Lisa

Josh and Lisa at a Yankees Game in 2017

Steve & younger brother Scott

Steve, Lisa, and Steve's Grandmother Mary at Steve's
college graduation

Steve, Lisa, and Josh (as a baby)

Steve, Lisa with his mother Bonnie with her second
husband Alan Goldberg at Steve and Lisa's wedding in
1990

Steve and Lisa's wedding photo (1990)

Top Left to Right: David Gordon, April Castagna, Bill Dichello, Paul Ryder, Hilary Spain-Reilly, Scott Grove.

Middle Left to Right: Marc Patten, Helene Thau-Lieberman, Kathy Iannazzo, Chuck Sullivan.

Bottom Left to Right: Lisa Ginsburg-Cleveland, Pam Gerrol

Steve, Scott, and Bonnie after Steve's College Graduation from Quinnipiac University.

Having earned the Eagle Scout Award in

1979

and desiring to continue to
promote, support, and apply
Scouting ideals through service.

Steven M. Grove

is hereby recognized by the

National Eagle Scout Association

as a member in good standing
through the year.

1997

Steve Grove Eagle Scout Award
(Recognized for good standing on award years later)

Steve, Lisa, and Josh family photo

Josh (in middle school) with Dennis (his grandfather) at bring your dad to work day

Dennis Grove, Josh with Scott's kids' cousins Meghan, Brendan, and Kiera Grove (left to right) (Taken after Steve passed away)

GROVE, STEVEN

June 20, 2003, Steven Grove of 101 Sky view Circle, Hamden beloved husband of Lisa Patten Grove Loving son and step-son of Bonnie and Alan Goldberg of Hamden. Dear father of Joshua Adam Grove of Hamden. Cherished brother of Scott Lawrence Grove of NJ and the late Lisa Beth Grove.

Funeral services in the Robert E. Shure Funeral Home, 543 George St., New Haven Sunday afternoon (TODAY) at 2:00 o'clock with interment services to follow in the Mishkan Israel Cemetery on Whalley Ave., New Haven. Memorial contributions maybe e sent to a charity of ones choice. A period of mourning will be observed at the family home thru Thursday.

Steve Grove's obituary

Scott, Kiera, Emily, and Josh at the University of South Carolina

(Where Kiera went to college) visiting for a weekend

Josh and his late grandmother Bonnie Goldberg

Josh with his Grandparents Peter and Sandra Patten (Left) and with Peter Raider (Stepfather), Uncle Marc Patten, and Grandfather Peter Patten (Right)

Josh and his family celebrating his grandfather Peter Patten's birthday. Pictured (right to left). Jolie Patten, Lisa Grove-Raider, Sandra Patten, Peter Patten, Rena Patten, and Marc Patten.

Josh and his fraternity in college at various charity events including
The Relay for Life (2013 - 2016)

Josh, Beverly Grove (Steve's Stepmother), Ben Wallace (NBA Hall-of-Famer) and Brendan Grove at a local charity event in Connecticut called "Special Olympics Dream Ride"

Josh, Emily, Melissa Coluccio and Max Holm on the day of our engagement, Summer, 2022

Lisa & Peter Raider (Josh's stepfather) dropping Josh off at the University at Buffalo (2013)

Andy Chasanoff, Max Holm, and Dan Fishman (Left to Right) at Max Holm and Melissa Coluccio's wedding in 2022

Josh and his fiancé Emily Seitz at a wedding in 2019

Chapter 9: Human Nature, Part 1

Steve Grove:

The real reason I thought about documenting my own experience with cancer is because of what it has revealed to me about human nature. Most of these experiences could be prefaced by, "I would never believe this was true if it hadn't happened to me." I couldn't possibly make up these stories, no matter how rich of an imagination I may have.

Soon after I began to tell people of my findings, the calls and visits started. People are so well-meaning, but you won't believe how they act in such situations, the stories that people feel the need to tell you, and how much you have to hold people up. I suppose you are wondering about that statement. The truth is that people look to you as the sick person for a sign and signal. Their reactions and feelings depend on your reactions and feelings. So, when people come to see you, they are looking to feel better about your situation. You may feel completely terrible, lousy, and awful, but your loved ones need a sign. They need to have relief from the burden of the disease. I asked my former Rabbi about this. We have been friends for many years and, although we no longer belong to his synagogue – it is too far a drive from our home – we remain close and in touch. He told me that when soldiers go into battle, their families are often in much worse shape psychologically than they are.

When you are in a battle, you are just worrying about that and getting out of it. That is your only focus. And if something goes wrong, there isn't anything that you can do. Your loved ones, however, remain worried about what is going on and hope that nothing bad will happen. They also worry about something happening to them. I suppose that this makes sense; even so, I still wonder why I had to hold everyone up.

Josh Grove:

Dealing with a family member getting cancer is not easy. It was tough on my family and on me, and our friends and relatives. I started this book because I did not wish to bury my head in the sand and forget about my father's battle, about everything he – and we as a family – went through. I felt it was on me to continue Steve's fight for the truth, to ask the right questions. I was always curious about how my father was diagnosed, how he coped with the treatments, and how he dealt with it psychologically. I also wondered how the disease he carried could potentially affect me or my future. And I knew that the only way to get those answers was to try and ask the right questions, by which I mean, the tough questions. As I continued to do this, and stayed the course, I knew that if I could reach even one person, I would create lasting effects that could help not just me but many more people struggling with a similar situation.

But not everyone feels that way. When something is difficult, when a truth is hard to bear, people will usually try and run away from it. This is particularly true of cancer, which is a difficult topic for many, and maybe even something of a taboo topic in our society. My father shared that many people wanted to see him, and that while they wanted to be supportive of him, he would often end up being the one supporting them. He would try to boost their spirits and stay positive. Some people, of course, were offering support for the wrong reasons or had their own agendas; others were well-meaning and truly wanted to help. But no matter how empathetic a person is, they are, at the end of the day, also just trying to get by. When their friend, coworker, or relative gets cancer, they want to feel reassured. They want to be told everything is going to work out. This is only human. Still, I believe there is a better way to approach such difficult situations. To anyone who reads this, I hope my father's words can provide some advice and guidance on how to be a better support giver. Whether someone you know is dealing with cancer or another problem, I encourage you to face the facts and make a plan for dealing with your feelings, rather than trying to find the easy way out or seeking false reassurance from the person who is suffering.

Steve Grove:

As I began telling people about my disease, the whole world needed to see that I was doing well, that I had a good attitude, and that things were moving forward positively. To be perfectly honest, I never was quite sure why I found myself being the cheerleader. Even when things were going badly, here I was, Steve, the Magic Colon Cancer Cheerleader! The better I felt about things, the more positive everyone around me seemed to be. I didn't know when there would be time to fall apart. Perhaps I wasn't supposed to, and that would have just made matters worse. In any case, I remained strong right up until the operating room. I do have a positive attitude about things, and if you are reading this because you are sick, you might need to do that also. You will need to be strong for yourself and others. Life is certainly for the living, and those who are happy want to stay happy.

This is not a bad thing; it is just reality. You have to tell everyone that you are going to be all right and that things are going better each day. I got tired a lot, especially while I was recuperating from the surgery, but people needed to see and know that I was doing better. Sorry, you'll have to be a cheerleader. You have to understand that you are essentially holding up the earth like Atlas, the Greek figure. You will have to receive people when they have the time to visit and accept their support when they are in a position to give it.

Another thing you have to be prepared for are the stories; everyone is going to tell you theirs. And many of these stories will be very sad ones. I often laughed as people would go into these long and drawn-out tales of other people getting very sick where, in the end, they would drop dead. Yes, amazingly, people will end on this "cheerful" note!

You don't need to hear these stories. Be prepared to give people a rule. Tell them you read this rule in this book. The rule is simple: no story unless it has a happy ending. I got so tired of listening to depressing stories, or sometimes just depressing people, after a while. You know those people. I'm sure you have them in your life also. Just try to stop them before they get into the gory details. If someone manages to slip the story by you – and trust me, they will – you'll simply have to laugh it off.

Josh Grove:

In a previous chapter, my father asked himself "Why me? Why did I have to get cancer?" In the end, he decided that there was no point in asking this question; that had been his lot in life, and he had to deal with it the best he could. And he does the same here. While he questioned why he had to be "the cheerleader" who held people up throughout his treatment process, in the end, he embraced the role. My father was a selfless person who always put others first. I don't believe he was bitter about having to stay positive. It may have tired him, but he made a plan for dealing with it. He made up rules to help him cope and better fulfill his assigned role (e.g., no story unless it has a happy ending).

We all do things we may not want to do. We do them because we are asked to at work, because we wish to achieve a goal we have set ourselves, or because we wish to help others. It's a part of life. This may be a cliché, but it does have multiple layers of meaning. Even when we are feeling down in the dumps, or tired, or overwhelmed, we must remember that other people's feelings are as acutely felt as ours. We must do our best to be there for them. My father did this even when he was feeling worse than them; he tried to be cheerful and positive. Although Steve had a tough time understanding why people would do things like call his hospital room after 8 p.m., ultimately, he knew in his heart that comforting and reassuring those of his friends who needed it was the right thing to do. You never know what someone is dealing with privately. You will come across many different kinds of people, all with various backgrounds, motives, and emotional scars. Steve knew that giving them attention and cheering them up was both for his own benefit as well as their own: he wanted to help people who were struggling so that they could in turn support him and help him stay positive.

Steve Grove:

People are also nosy. I mean that in a nice and friendly way, but it is true. They will start asking very detailed questions about your surgery and treatments. "Tell me how the preparation for the colonoscopy went." You would not believe how many questions like that you get. You can stop them pretty quickly by getting extremely graphic. "Well, the liquid I drank tastes like rotten milk with a tiny bit of sugar added in to kill the taste. I then proceeded to have projectile diarrhea so extensive that it would have spanned 10 to 15 feet if I had been laid horizontally." It's at this point that you see them feel sorry they ever asked, and that is when you can go in for the kill: "The diarrhea only lasted eight hours, with some small residuals for about ten hours after that... now do you understand?"

I know it may sound cruel, but people will ask the most incredible things. I even had people ask about the location and type

113

of scar I had after my surgery. "Where did they cut? What type of knife did they use? Do you have a scar? Did they shave you?" I was almost waiting for the next question to be "Can I see it?" People have always had an interest in the gory and the grisly. Why do you think people slow down for accidents? Why are scary movies so popular? We can't let our imagination work any longer, we have to see, know, hear, and understand. Well, to be perfectly honest, I didn't even want to look at my incision. It was only a reminder of someone cutting me open and sticking their hands inside my body. That doesn't seem normal to me.

Although it goes on all the time, I still can't imagine why a person would want to do that. I know that science has advanced, and we are an amazingly healthy society now because of it, but the facts are still quite simple. One person cuts another person open and puts his or her hands inside them. All I can say is… yuck. I had to tell the story of my procedure at all times of the day, in person, to friends, family, and even just people I did business with. I told this story so well that I could have done it in my sleep. You'll have to do the same. People want to know the exact nature of what you have, where it is, what the doctors are doing, how they are doing it, and what happens after. So if people want to know, then answer them. I guess I didn't watch when Katie Couric had her colonoscopy on the Today Show because I have a hard enough time getting up in the morning and getting going. I am sure it was interesting, and someone even told me that I could go on the internet and see it over and over again. I think people who do that are very courageous; I just didn't feel up to watching it or posting my experience on the world wide web.

Josh Grove:

It's truly impressive how many contradictory roles you have to hold as the sick person. You are trying not to think too much about the unpleasant realities of the disease or the surgical procedures, while at the same time you have to satisfy people's curiosity and talk about those aspects of the illness. You have to stay positive in order not to bring people down, but also listen to people's morbid stories about their own sick or dead relatives—which might make it, in fact, harder for you to stay positive. I can see here a few coping strategies my father developed in order to deal with these contradictions. First and foremost, he tried to answer people's questions honestly. But when dealing with certain types of people, he may not always have had the right answers, or else found that their questions were crossing the boundary from "curious" into "nosy." That is where his famous dry humor came in.

Steve Grove:

The most amazing part of my disease is how people just don't know what to say. They don't know if they should be happy about the fact that you are getting better; they don't know if they should be sad about you being sick; they just don't know. The funniest moments happened when people didn't know how to react, so they decided to tell me a story.

The story always started out the same: "You'll never believe it, but my aunt's neighbor's son's mother-in-law's boss's friend had the same disease about 10 years ago." Well, so far, I am listening and barely believing it, but I am listening. "They had this disease, and it went on for ages and ages and… Oh, oh, oh! And they died from it!" At that point, I would look for Allen Funt and the Candid Camera crew. There had to be a camera around, as this person would then burst into sobs and go on and on about how terrible things were.

I am talking about intelligent people here. I am talking about close friends and family members. They all told me these stories, and many of them ended in bad news. I suppose the obvious question for me was, "Why would I want to listen to this babbling in the condition I am in?" I needed people to be quiet, just hug me, listen, laugh, and smile, and then go away quickly. That was all. You'll find people always feel that they have to talk. People either don't keep quiet when they should, or they don't say anything at all. That was even more "fun"—the visits where I had to carry the entire conversation. So, for all of you reading this, here are some of my suggested rules:

- *Don't tell stories that end in bad news.*

- *Sit with your friend and hold them, hug them, kiss them, and just relax.*

- *Tell jokes, talk about your life, talk about their lives, and talk about the weather.*

- *Don't sit silently and make them come up with subjects to talk about; bring a list of subjects if you have to.*

- *Don't make a pest of yourself.*

The other interesting part that told me a lot about human behavior was people's need to make contact. I wasn't home for one day and the phone went crazy. The first week out of hospital was the same. In addition, this is the time when you'll need to rest and relax and when you won't feel like talking. There should not be any phones in hospital rooms. You are spaced out on narcotics, you are in pain, there are tubes everywhere, you can barely reach the phone, and it rings and rings... You would not believe it, but I actually had several calls after 10 PM in the hospital room. I was wondering what they thought I was doing. Did my friends and family think I was sitting up, watching Dateline, and eating some ice cream? Most nights by 8 PM I was zonked out cold and awaiting my next wake-up call to check if I was sleeping. You may laugh at that, but it happens time and time again. People need to call, of course, just not after 8 PM!

People feel the need to help, and sometimes they do it on their terms and not yours. They will visit you despite your inability to even recognize their presence. You may or may not be receptive to their help at the times when it is being given. That is how it goes. When you are feeling well but feeling lonely, there isn't anyone around. The second you feel tired, sit down to rest or feel a bit sick, the phone and doorbell will not stop ringing.

Again, people want to know how you are so they can stop worrying. They don't like to feel anxious or upset, so contacting you and driving you nuts with their calls is their way of making themselves feel better. I know it sounds harsh but be prepared. The flood is not welcomed, but it will happen. Oh yes, and everyone will start with, "I know you don't feel like talking, or it's hard to talk, so I'll just be a minute." I counted 48 calls like that in five days in the hospital. The number should have been unlisted.

I don't want to sound cynical or ungrateful. The support we received from friends and family was wonderful and welcomed.

116

Knowing how many people were truly interested and cared truly gave us strength. The only issue was the volume at a time when you didn't ask for it. It's a lot to handle all at once.

Josh Grove:

So, a friend is telling you a story about something that is affecting them. As you are listening, based on their tone, their words, their body language and your relationship with them, you might be skeptical, or empathetic, or indifferent. Regardless, you will form your own opinion and try to relate to the story in some way. It's only natural that you will want to give some sort of advice, whether your friend wants or is able to take your advice. You may also react in a way that you are embarrassed of, afterwards. I encourage you to think back to a situation where someone's words or actions caused you to react differently than you would have wanted; it probably was out of discomfort or because you were feeling awkward. It's human nature, right?

Cancer is still one of the most uncomfortable topics to discuss even in today's society, so it is not surprising that, as Steve describes above, many people do not know how to talk about it, or have difficulty finding something helpful to say. When you are affected by cancer, there is no right way to explain how it feels; perhaps it is impossible for other people to understand. Yet people try to help. They try to give you advice. They may even project their anxiety about you in a way that may become frustrating, such as advising you to "Just relax!" or repeatedly asking "What can I do?" and "How are you feeling?" They also give you their stories in the hope that you can relate to them and that they will give you comfort. These stories are ones that many families deal with: a sick relative, or a friend they once had who fought the same battle. They are the stories that my father listened to again and again. And sometimes, it got exhausting.

My father had an incredible ability to form a connection with *anyone*. While writing this story and reading my father's writings, I have taken pride in his ability to develop lifelong relationships and put in the work to maintain them. However, cancer is a test of most people's kindness and patience. Knowing how to deal with people in this kind of situation is not easy, nor does it come with a handy instruction manual to guide you. In life, you will come across many different people with distinct and sometimes difficult personalities.

117

This is already complex to navigate when you are feeling at your best, let alone when you are, as my father calls it, "zonked out cold" by medication.

I also found this often when talking to others about my father, when trying to explain who he was, what he went through, and how his disease and death impacted me and my family. This was once a touchy and awkward subject for me, and I would sometimes get irritated with people who didn't "get it." But I chose to use this as an opportunity for growth. With time, I slowly improved on this front. I changed the way in which I talk to people about my father. I learned to cut as much of the awkwardness out of the conversation as possible. I wanted to make sure others did not feel uncomfortable, but I also wanted to tell the truth and not skate over the stark reality of what it means to deal with cancer in your family. It is a skill you can practice and I continue to work on it every time I tell my father's story.

Yes, some people will not know what to say; some people will be awkward; and some will be downright unhelpful. But being able to deal with various personality types, uncomfortable situations, and conversations is a skill that will serve you well in life. It will put you one step closer to achieving your goals. It has certainly helped me, in more ways than I can count. Having dealt with many people throughout this process has tested both my emotions and my mental capacity; it has helped me become a better, kinder, and more well-rounded person. So it would appear my father was right when he told me, "Something good can always come out of something bad."

Steve Grove:

I have lost a lot of weight in this process. I have lost a total of 35 pounds in the past three months and probably can afford to lose another 20 or so. Another 20 or so will put me at my high school weight and size. I imagine that I'll never be that size again, as gravity hasn't helped matters, but I don't mind trying and seeing what I will look like. It's funny. So many people have said to me, "How can I catch what you have?" or "Can you bottle that for me?" I know that this is all meant in jest, but I have to sit back in amazement that anyone could even envy for a second the results of the nature of what I have happening to me.

On the other hand, I was heavy and will no longer be. I have resolved to keep this weight off and be healthier. That's a good thing as a result of this illness. We are an overweight society. There are restaurants where the portions served to one person would feed an entire family for a week in some parts of the world. We eat too much, and we are too fat. I am happy to believe that this process has changed me, and maybe it has given others the motivation they needed also to change. (But to the general reading public, I am not bottling and selling my disease so others can lose weight!)

Chapter 10: Human Nature, Part 2

Steve Grove:

People are going to feel helpless. Most people can't heal or help you, so they want to do something. My suggestion is to be practical. Ask them to help with important things; give them things to do that you will need. If people want to help, send them shopping for groceries, get them to pick up medication, or have them babysit. Ask them to come to your house and cut the grass, stain the deck, or fertilize the lawn. We lined up a bunch of people to help when things were hardest, and things worked out fine. I was up and around within a few days of surgery, and I was home and feeling better in a matter of weeks. I tried to ask people to hold off getting me gifts and baskets and, instead, asked for prepared meals from a caterer or kosher market. This was quite helpful. You'll need to make your life simple and easy as you deal with everything else you have to take care of. Again, people who love you are going to want to help. Let them do things that matter in your life.

Josh Grove:

I've always been someone who has preferred to take care of my own problems rather than delegate them to someone else. My mentality was: "If you want something done right, do it yourself." This is a quality that my father shared as well. He was a very self-sufficient person who did not like to depend on others. However, being able to take care of yourself and maintaining that do-it-alone mentality is much easier said than done when you are sick. Overcoming the many roadblocks and setbacks that cancer throws at you is not easy. Even daily chores and simple tasks can feel like a high mountain to climb. It can be hard to learn to accept help and reach out to your community. But my father found ways to do so, and do so gracefully and gratefully.

Steve Grove:

People are going to react differently to you and your illness. You are going to have those who are right there asking loads of questions and others who are very silent. Some close friends will avoid you because they just don't know what to say. You are going to have to help them. Tell them to just love you and listen, talk, and laugh. Have people help you pass the time. That is a good start. You'll recuperate slowly, and this will involve a lot of resting. You'll get tired easily. Communicate this to your friends. There is nothing wrong with telling them the truth and letting them support you.

How will you stay in touch with people who want to know how you are? I found that some mass emailing worked quite well. People were so happy to hear about what was going on and to know that our attitude was positive. You may feel the need and tendency to shrink back, tell no one, and just suffer. Try to fight that. It is important for many reasons to share your condition with others who truly care and love you. Their love will help. Their well wishes and funny stories will help. The community at large will reach out and assist, and you will feel better after having told people what the story is.

People will want you to keep them in the loop, but don't feel bad if you can't. Call those people when you have a chance and use email if you can. You can reach a bunch of people quickly and then know that they are notified of what is happening. I am sure I will keep my email contact list posted on what is happening as often as possible. I can tell who has and hasn't responded, and sometimes I have been surprised. I know that many people stayed by my side who I never thought I would hear from and who had never called before. It will be that way; just accept it.

Josh Grove:

"Just accept it." This is something that comes up again and again in Steve's writing. One of the toughest things to do is to accept what we can and cannot control, as my father mentioned previously. He wrote that life is divided into three parts: one third is luck, one third is attitude, and one third is everything else. Ultimately learning to *control the controllable* will become your biggest asset, one that I firmly believe is crucial in overcoming struggle and achieving your goals. It is especially applicable when dealing with family members who are diagnosed with a deadly disease such as cancer, where there are so many things you cannot control. My father always wanted to please everyone during his treatment process. He described it almost like lifting guilt from his shoulders. I'm sure everyone has had that feeling at one time or another. From personal experience, it never

121

works. Do what you can to uplift others, to connect with them, and leave the rest up to them. Control not only what you can, but what you are comfortable with. Ultimately, leave what you feel is not controllable up to fate and let life take its course, one day at a time.

Embracing the concept of luck and being able to leave some things up to chance is not something that comes easy to everyone, myself included. But the fact is there is a small percentage that you can control in life, even when you are healthy, able, and determined. There will always be aspects of life that you cannot do anything about, whether that is gaining weight, losing your hair, or your job, getting sick... My father shows us how to deal with this. He accepted that which he could not change (e.g., that people needed contact and insisted on being allowed to help him) and he did what he could to control the controllable (he found ways of contacting people on his own terms; he gave people who wanted to help practical things to do, setting his own rules), while leaving the rest up to chance and fate.

Try to take control of the few things you can stay in control of. As for everything else? "Let God take the wheel," and remember to be grateful for any luck or assistance that comes your way. When someone truly offers their support and kindness, when they reach out to you or extend a helping hand, you should grab on and hold tight.

Steve Grove:

The doctors told me to rest when I got home, and I did an awful lot of that, but I also did a lot of entertaining, among other things. Again, be prepared for this. Often, I would be the one to ask, "Can I get you something to drink or eat?"

Let me talk to you about gifts also. You will get more gifts than you know what to do with. The flowers, plants, food baskets, and fruit baskets will come to the hospital and your home until you can't stand to look at another kiwi fruit. Remember that the gifts are a nice way for people to say that they are thinking of you. The food and fruit will most likely be things you have to avoid for a while, but the plants and flowers will add some color to your life. It will also be fun to talk to the delivery people who come. You'll be amazed how seeing another person becomes so important during the days when you are resting at home alone. No sarcasm or comedy here! This was a nice part of resting at home.

122

Josh Grove:

When people would come to visit my father, he wanted them to know that, despite being ill, he was going to continue to fight. So he put on his brave face and even did some "entertaining." If he was at times overwhelmed by people's need for contact at a time when he was feeling bad, he also learned to view it as positive and accept the gifts and offers to help for what they were: a way for people to show that they cared. He made a conscious decision to remain grateful and positive. His mentality, even at the end, was "How can something good come out of this?"

Whether you are affected by this terrible disease or not, try to look inward and see how this story can be helpful to you. Think of aspects of your own life, from your job to your relationship with your significant other, and finally to your friends, family, and community. Perhaps one of them is causing you problems; perhaps you are in a pickle and do not know how to move forward. Ask yourself, is this story applicable to my own life? Can I learn something from this? An attitude? A coping mechanism? A way to gracefully decline or accept help? Who knows, maybe it will inspire you to work on yourself or to reach out. Even if you are only able to take the smallest bit out of this story, I will feel that I have done my part. Always remember, decision-making comes from your inner being, and it is a conscious process. You must decide to do something in order to make a positive change.

There is no manual to life. No one is going to explain to you what you should be doing with your life, how to react to any situation, and what kind of person you should be. That is for you to figure out on your own. Life is about making decisions, which may not necessarily always be the right ones. But they must be conscious ones, and driven by your own inner voice, your own goals, and purpose. No two random people are the same in how they discover their own purpose, their personal *why*. You can listen to people's advice—my father definitely believed that seeing your problem from another's perspective was helpful. But at the end of the day, the only thing that matters is that you decide for yourself. Do it. Make a conscious choice to make a change. Your future self will be sending you gift baskets.

Chapter 11: Sickness, Work, and Purpose

Steve Grove:

I am a working person. That means that I go to work, I earn money, I put it in my checking account, I make my car and mortgage payments, and I go back to work the next day. The one comment you will hear from everyone is "Don't worry and everything will work out." I am not discounting nor doubting those statements, but CUT IT OUT. I had a hard time with this and even snapped at people when they tried to tell me to relax, when I had all these worries. These words are spoken by people who continued to do their jobs and continued to receive their paychecks every pay period. But sometimes people get sick, and things don't work out.

I recently completed two years as President of the National Kidney Foundation (NKF) of Connecticut. I have kidney disease on top of everything else and have been active with our local NKF affiliate to help raise awareness, money, and assistance. One of the things I had to do was to approve patient assistance requests when people needed a quick bank aid fix to pay for some expenses. I can tell you from that experience that people get sick, and people lose everything. I read month after month about poor people who had no money for rent, car payments, medications, heating oil, and the like. People needed money, they didn't have it, and they couldn't earn it. Now, I am not sure about your view of the American Dream, but in my view, two cars, a house, and clothing should be basic staples. I am not even talking about vacations or fancy properties. I am talking about the basics.

No, money is not important in life. Friends and family are much more important. However, the reality is that you need to buy groceries, and your friends and family are not going to come over every weekend to do that for you. You need to be able to stand on your own and take care of things for yourself. Perhaps you will be lucky enough to have a disability insurance that will pay your full salary while you are out sick. But trust me, this is a worry for many, and there is nothing wrong with it.

Josh Grove:

Stories about cancer often follow a certain mold. People express their admiration for cancer survivors and call their stories "inspiring" but often, as Steve remarked in previous chapters too, they do not want to hear about the harsher realities of the disease. There are certain aspects that get glossed over, or that are considered almost rude to discuss. When one talks about cancer, one mustn't mention such things as work leaves, paychecks, or any financial difficulties caused by dealing with the disease. These will magically sort themselves out and are best swept under the carpet for now to focus on the recovery process. But of course, that is now how humans work. These worries continue to plague us, whether we want to or not. Once again, I appreciate and admire my father's bravery in bringing these issues to the forefront and discussing them openly.

Steve Grove:

After you are told you are ill, you try to prepare yourself and your world for some long-term time off. I own my business and know that I would probably never take five weeks off in a row for vacation—well, perhaps several years from now if I decide to drive across the country, but definitely not in the near future. Many things fill your head. What do I do first, second, third? How do I protect everything, insulate everything, and guarantee that there will be no issues while I am away? The truth is, you can't.

Many of my most interesting conversations were with some of my customers. Many of these customers have been customers and friends for years. Some of the projects we had with them were routine, and some were important with looming deadlines. What could I do, however? It's not like I had planned things this way. So I contacted them and told them, "I just want to let you know that I am sick and will be out for the next month or so." Most reacted in this way: "No problem, take care of yourself. The other guys in your office will take care of me. Don't worry about me!" Sounds great, huh? There were, however, a few of the following conversations:

"Okay, take care of yourself..." – long, long, long pause – "...but when do you think my stuff will be done?"

Some people will truly care and stand by your side, and others won't care a bit. That's the hard truth about life. Our world is not designed for those who suffer; there isn't any real room for

125

being ill in it. You may wonder what I mean by that. It's simple. Just look around at your community one day and watch everything that is going on. There aren't a lot of sick people out there building the houses, delivering the mail, or working the till at the grocery store. Life is for the healthy. If you are sick and reading this, then you already know a lot of what I am telling you. I don't know of any bank that will cover your mortgage or car payment because you aren't feeling well. I don't know of any supermarket that will deliver this week's groceries for free, and the car insurance company wants their premium in order to cover you. I suppose that people can assist and make things easier, but life mostly goes on for those who can enjoy it. Even in your own family, life will carry on. People will go places, do things, and have experiences, while you will be relegated to rest and relaxation. You will wonder when you will be able to go back and do all that you did prior to getting sick. At times, this thought will make you feel quite lonely. Life needs a purpose.

Josh Grove:

There are many lessons I have taken from my father. He taught me as a young kid that life is fragile, that I need to live my life to the fullest. He taught me to appreciate every moment with the people who mean the most to me and support those who matter most, because you never know when that last moment will come. But one of the most important lessons I have learned from him is to set goals in life and never give up on them. He always stressed that it was important for me to find a purpose that will steer me not just in the next month or year, but that will guide everything I do. From his work to his daily routines to his long-term financial goals, there was meaning and intention behind everything he did.

I can remember after my dad survived cancer for the first time, he continued to be involved in my life and extracurricular activities. He showed up for me. He was not going to let cancer stop him from trying to live his life. He wanted to continue his everyday routines and keep being a part of the world. But as the cancer progressed, this became harder to do. "*Life needs a purpose,*" he writes, yet the disease had started stripping him of all those things that gave purpose to his. Internally, it's clear he was struggling a lot with feeling alienated from the world around him. There is almost a sense here of separating the world into the sick and the healthy, and he had suddenly been relegated to the first category. Life was moving on, and he was getting left behind. He wasn't sure how to deal with it. It didn't help that he was not able to work. Steve was always a multi-tasker, a person involved in multiple projects and organizations, a community leader... Take all that away, and I can only wonder: how did he cope emotionally?

Let's re-read that last phrase for a moment: *"Life needs a purpose."* Take a second to let that sink in. Then ask yourself what it means to you. Do you agree with it? If so, what would you say is your life's purpose? What is your *why* for doing what you do? Do you know? If not, does this make you question anything?

Steve Grove:

Being sick just feels like you are taken out of the game in the first inning, despite your interest and past ability. People gave me advice to rest, relax, stay home, and don't worry about work. Well, my work is important to me. It's certainly important to me not to lose all that I have built, and it's important to me to have a purpose. I have my own accounting and consulting firm that I started about ten years ago. I like my job, love my employees, and enjoy my customers. My work is my passion and it's a part of me. Don't listen to people who insist that you rest and relax forever. Rest and relax as you need to, but keep your mind working and your passions burning. You need to have a purpose and a place to be. No matter what your work is, get back to it as soon as you can. It will help pass the time, and it will help keep things in perspective. And of course, it will pay the bills.

Josh Grove:

My father and I have similar feelings about the word "relax." That is to say, it is far from my favorite word. What does it mean, to "relax"? It means to become less stressed or anxious. Articulated in such a way, you realize it stands in opposition to two very loaded words. But anxiety comes from your head, as does stress... see what I'm getting at? To be able to "relax" you must make a conscious decision, in your mind, to tackle that which is causing you stress and anxiety. I have never found it very helpful to be told to just "relax"; I have always preferred to identify the problem, the source of my anxiety, then tackle it. But then again, I have never had cancer.

If you are a fighter, a doer, a go-getter, if you are as energetic a person as my father was, it can be hard to watch from the sidelines. Steve loved his job and loved his life. Getting sick, he wrote, felt like being "taken out of the game in the first inning." He was unprepared for it. To stay with the baseball metaphor, life had thrown him a curveball. For baseball fans out there, there are many different types of curveballs. There is the 12–6 curveball, which is simply like a clock and drops from 12 to 6 on the dot; there is the knuckle curve, which comes to the batter at an angle that is hard to pick up; and then there is the one you can't quite identify. This is called the "unknown pitch." What do you do when life throws you one of those?

For a while, Steve continued to express his hope that he would be able to get back to his regular activities and to his normal life as soon as possible. This felt necessary to him both for financial reasons and also for his mental wellbeing. But after a while he started to look at it in a different way. He acquired a new purpose. "When life throws you lemons you make beef stew," the comedian Andrew Milonakis once said. I read this variation on the popular quote as a young man, and it took me a long time to understand it. It makes a lot of sense to me now. Think about it: if you're planning to make lemonade, getting lemons is quite handy, isn't it? But in reality, life isn't that predictable. What you may get instead are random ingredients that don't quite fit whatever you had in mind—those unknown curveballs, in the previous analogy. You may have been planning on making lemonade, but now, you may need to re-think your plan. You need to use your skills and resources to come up with a new strategy, and sometimes, you need to think outside the box in order to do that. In other words, you may need to make beef stew, not lemonade!

And that is indeed what Steve did. My father was not able to get back to work entirely in the way that he wanted. But he found his "beef stew" eventually. He still needed to pay the bills, but the disease prevented him from working full-time. So he looked for another way. In Steve's last few years, he made peace with cancer. He would never say life wasn't fair, or wish he could walk in someone else's shoes because he had found a new purpose in life: to write this book and, in doing so, help others who were struggling with the same disease.

Steve Grove:

I wrote this book because I haven't worked much during the past few months, and I could always use some income. I have a terrible disability policy that only pays me for 90 days while I am totally disabled at about 30% of my salary and kicks in at 70% of my salary after 90 days if, and only if, I am totally disabled. My wife is a teacher and is teaching in a private school, so, to be honest, we hope the book will be picked up and published. I also wrote this book to help others. I hope that all who read it will see a little of themselves in it, whether they are the patient, friend, family, or just someone who "knows someone" (and in my experience, someone always knows someone who knows someone who has the disease you have).

I know that people may feel funny about talking to others about these things, but encourage them to do so, and encourage them to tell the truth! By being honest, you will help others. Early detection and treatment of cancer are very important, and you may just be the inspiration needed to help others move forward in a positive screening. I know that many people went out and got screened after they spoke to me and that made me feel good. If others can benefit, why not do something to help?

Josh Grove:

In starting to write what would become this book, Steve had found himself a new purpose: to help others. But it is important to note that he continued to keep hacking away at his main goal, which was to get healthy. His desire to help others only further fueled his determination to keep fighting, to conquer the disease. He wanted to finish the book and publish it. Keeping this forward-thinking and goal-focused mentality was critical to his sanity and emotional well-being. It would help him stay positive, which in turn would help him to overcome this sickness. He really believed he could beat cancer.

There will always be ebbs and flows in life; times when we drift away from our goals and from others, and times when we feel a sense of connection and purpose. For me, becoming a part of the Relay for Life community was such a turning point. For those who are unfamiliar with Relay for Life, it is a twenty-four-hour marathon walk where you take part in various activities throughout the day and night to raise money for The American Cancer Society. Those participating can either camp or have a site together with a team, while everyone takes turns walking for a full day. I can't tell you how much these events have done for me and my family. Having the opportunity to be with other people you can relate to and who are in a similar situation as you, sharing your stories and listening to theirs will give you back a feeling of hope. It will make you feel that your story, your journey is *purposeful*. Looking back now, twenty years later, the Relay for Life community has had an enormous impact on my life, much bigger than I could have ever imagined or appreciated at the time. I urge you to get involved in such charity events in your own community. The magnitude of the event is not important; what is important is what you will give to others and what you will take from it.

My first Relay for Life was in 2002. I was nine years old at the time, but still, I can vividly remember my father speaking as a survivor, having beaten cancer for the first time. It was an important moment for our family. We all thought at that moment that we could conquer anything. I remember looking up at the stage, listening to my father as he gave his speech as a cancer survivor, and thinking how proud of him I was. He had not given up! He had beaten the disease! And even though the cancer returned, the feeling of pride in his perseverance has never left me. Steve was a fighter, and in his battle with cancer, he never, ever laid down his arms.

If you have a close family member or friend who is affected by cancer, always remember that, even though they may not show it, inside, that person is fighting as hard as they can to keep going. So, you should, too. You owe it to them to never stop the fight. And try to remember: it's not how hard you get hit, but how hard you get up and hit back. Twenty years have passed since my father expressed his desire that this book be published, and here I am, all this time later, taking up the baton and finally finishing the project he dedicated the last years of his life to. I thought to myself: I am my father's son. I owe it to him to never stop the fight.

Chapter 12: Adventures in a Broken System

Josh Grove:

I want to preface this chapter by making a crucial distinction: being *sick* with cancer versus being affected by it are two completely different things. As I sit here and write this, I cannot say that I have ever been sick with cancer, though being so close to it has had a huge impact on me and my way of thinking. For me, this book is more than simply a story about cancer; its scope is wider than that. If it does not sound too grandiose to say so, I believe the book is really about the meaning of life. In my own sections, I have focused less on dissecting the various treatments my father underwent chronologically, less on the day-to-day details of his disease, and more on the lessons that can be derived from his story. How does one become a person of integrity and honor? What constitutes a life well-lived, a life lived with purpose? What, I wondered, can I and others learn from Steve about perseverance and patience, gratitude, and kindness, about faith and hope?

But of course, when you are the one battling illness, it's hard not to become absorbed in those very details and to avoid feeling frustrated and overwhelmed by the treatment and recovery process. For the person who is sick, the daily battle against cancer is all there is. This chapter delves deeper into Steve's remarkable journey as he makes his way through a labyrinth of appointments, medical procedures, and "alternative" treatments, and sheds light on the frustrations he encountered while seeking the care he deserved.

Steve Grove:

If you've never been sick, then you have never been involved with the "healing" community. I think it's a culture within our culture. You just won't believe the types of cures that you can find out there. I will keep adding to this section as I heal and finish up my treatments, but you'll be tested from the first minute. Remember, I told you earlier that people are going to offer advice. Well, I'll just list some of the highlights of the advice. Add your own as you get it:

- *"Shark cartilage seems to work if you suck on it."*

- *"Chew on various roots from trees and plants."*

- *"Go see a faith healer and postpone your surgery."*

- *"Convert to being Catholic so Jesus can save you." (We are conservative Jews, and are quite faithful and observant.)*

Josh Grove:

Remember how I talked about Steve trying to find the humor in any situation? Well, that list of advice is Steve's dry humor, at its peak. The advice to convert to Catholicism in order to be saved by Jesus is even funnier when you realize Jesus was Jewish.

Steve Grove:

You may be reading this and thinking, "So what? They are good ideas. Try them!" I believe in outside consultations and second opinions. I have been a career-focused individual my whole life, so I can appreciate people who question things and who are open to new ideas. In my profession, no one accountant has all the answers, and the same is true for doctors. No one infuses all the information in the world into any physician, so check them out, ask questions, and go get that second opinion. I want to know from others if I am on target or off my rocker. At this stage, the count of those who tell me I am on target and those who say I am off my rocker is running neck and neck. You have many choices when you are faced with a disease. The physicians will help explain these choices, but ultimately, you will have to make the decisions along the way.

Josh Grove:

Over the years, I've been in many situations where I was convinced that I didn't need anyone's advice. Whether my problems pertained to personal matters, my career, or family decisions, I would attempt to solve them on my own. But in time, I came to recognize the wisdom of seeking a second opinion. I started listening to advice, albeit maintaining some degree of skepticism. This shift in perspective gradually taught me that seeking input from trusted professionals or loved ones can provide valuable insights and allow you to see the bigger picture and make informed choices in pivotal moments. Of course, there are moments when going with your instincts might be the right path. It's a delicate balance, knowing when to rely on others' advice and when to trust your own intuition, knowledge, and experience. But this high-risk, high-reward equation tends to work in your favor when you open yourself up to new ideas and thoughtfully assess your options before making a decision.

My father also faced a crucial decision over two decades ago when he sought guidance from cancer specialists. He chose to consult multiple experts, recognizing that getting the information and then weighing his options would increase his knowledge and, ultimately, his chances of survival. He also consulted with members of what he called "the healing community" and other cancer sufferers. Getting a second opinion was a principle he held dearly, not only when it came to medical decisions but also in dealings with attorneys and family matters. He sought advice from everyone and anyone. He was determined to make the best decisions for his own survival. Some might say that asking others for counsel shows vulnerability or weakness. However, I believe it shows mental fortitude. The ability to seek the most valuable advice and decide which to follow and which to discard is a strength. Developing the patience and mental resilience to do this, even when it doesn't always lead to your desired outcomes, can bring a newfound belief in yourself. This self-belief not only strengthens your own resolve but also inspires others to believe in you. Sometimes, you have to take that leap of faith. As Michael Jordan once said, "You miss 100% of the shots you don't take." So, if you don't venture into the unknown, you'll never discover what could have been.

One of Steve's peers, speaking to me as part of the research for this book, described him as "mature beyond his years." But what does it mean to be "mature" or wise? I think that this openness to others that Steve showed again and again, his ability to view his life from another's viewpoint, holds part of the answer. As you grow up, you start to pick up on certain things you may not have when you were younger. This evolving perception accompanies your journey into adulthood. The way you view yourself and how others view you profoundly affects how you navigate significant life events. The phrase "perception is reality" means that everything you experience, including thoughts, emotions, and sensations, is filtered through the lens of your personal experiences and conditioning. Your understanding of the world is not the world as it is, but rather your perception of it. It's essential to recognize that your family, friends, and colleagues, although experiencing the same situations, may have a completely different take on them. Neither of you is wrong; your perspectives simply reflect individual perceptions of reality. Take a minute to let that sink in. What can it teach you about empathy? What can it teach you about listening to others' viewpoints?

I invite you here to pause and reflect on any past disagreements or conflicts you may have had with friends or family. Perhaps you thought you were in the right in an argument and have held onto grudges over time. One thing I learned from my father is that life is short; too short to sweat the small stuff. So, as you are sitting there reading this and wondering how this relates to your life, I encourage you to attempt looking at your differences from that person's perspective. Their point of view may help you with your own problem, and may also give you the tools and compassion you need to overcome the differences you have had in the past. Or it may not; you may still not agree with them. Regardless, knowing you made the effort to consider both sides will give you peace of mind.

As you will read about my father's encounters with people in the medical field, you will come across some opinions you may or may not agree with. You might think to yourself, "I would have reacted differently in that situation." Try and look at the bigger picture. Acknowledge that this is Steve's personal experience and try to put yourself in his shoes.

Steve Grove:

We made the long trip for a weekend up to the Dana Farber Cancer Center in Boston, Massachusetts. I highly recommend it if you have cancer. This is a beautiful place with specialists in every corner. They'll do a great job of listening to you. I hear that the Sloan Kettering Memorial Cancer Center in New York is much the same. No matter where you live, if you can find a cancer center, go get a second opinion. I am lucky that what I have as cancer and a spread were dealt with quickly and seem to be treatable. Plus, my local oncologist was given the seal of approval at Dana Farber. My doctor encouraged us to get a second opinion, and we saw a specialist who confirmed what we were being told on a local level.

Josh Grove:

The Dana Farber Cancer Center in Boston, Massachusetts is amongst the best cancer research centers in the United States. A year or so after my father got diagnosed, he decided to visit an oncologist at this center. This is around 2001–2002. My father had heard good things about the center, and he wanted to get another opinion after what he had been told by his local doctors in New Haven. He knew that he might walk away from the center with bad news, or a potentially worse prognosis, but he realized it was in his own best interest to pay them a visit. He decided to risk it.

The visit paid off. It confirmed my father's diagnosis and offered him additional information on where to go from there. The war against the disease was about to start, and he was preparing himself for the first battle. The confirmation of his diagnosis would be the beginning of many doctor visits, procedures, and surgeries – and on top of that, many administrative hassles and bureaucratic challenges that left him feeling frustrated and tired.

Steve Grove:

This system is broken, and it has to be fixed. There are many shining stars within it, but you won't believe some of the things you experience. "The doctor will see patients Tuesday morning from 10:00 to 12:00, Thursday from 2:00 to 5:00, and every other Friday." That's what I heard when I first called one of my doctors for an appointment. "Well, I am trying to work a bit before going into the hospital, and seeing as I'll be out for a while, is there any flexibility?" I asked. "No, the doctor is very busy." I thought for a bit and told them I would call back. I tried to rearrange my schedule, and when I did call back, I got the answering service: "The office is closed for lunch from 12:00 to 1:30, unless it's an emergency. Call back after that." Click. I listened and marveled at the office's ability to take a lunch break and turn everything off. Everyone in my doctor's office is like that. I only wish I was able to take a lunch break like that. I can see it now: "The accounting offices of Steven Grove are closed for lunch from noon to 1:30. Please call back after that." Why don't I think that would ever work? I called back and negotiated an appointment with the secretary, who must have worked in the White House because I think getting in to see the

President of the United States may be easier than getting in to see the various doctors.

Josh Grove:

Many years after my father wrote those words about his harrowing battle with cancer and the dysfunctional healthcare system he describes, I can't help but feel a mix of anger and frustration. Reading about his struggle to secure a doctor's appointment and the absurdity of their scheduling system is infuriating. It's a stark reminder of the many external challenges he had to contend with during those trying times, in addition to the physical pain and the psychological distress that comes with battling cancer. The way he humorously compares his own work schedule to the office's lunch break reflects his resilience and sense of humor even in the face of adversity. It's a testament to his strength that he managed to navigate this imperfect system.

One word that beautifully encapsulates my father's journey through treatment and his interactions with medical professionals is "patience." This is something that did not come easy to me growing up. I always wanted answers, and I wanted them right away. I had almost an anxious feeling when I was reading the part about my father frantically seeking information and answers when he was first diagnosed because it was so relatable, especially to my younger self. If you or a loved one have had an experience with cancer – or any kind of chronic illness – I'm certain that you, too, have encountered moments that truly test your patience. While I haven't had to grapple with healthcare bureaucracy and medical challenges in the same way my father did, I did learn a lot from how he dealt with these hurdles. The frustration he expresses here is not something I ever saw him show during his many years in and out of hospitals. I am in awe of the unwavering patience he displayed, even in the face of doubt and uncertainty. So, if you are going through a difficult time, try to tap into that reservoir of patience that you hold within you, as it's often the very key that unlocks the door to resilience and hope.

I want to take a moment here to address something you should keep in mind while you read about Steve's adventures in the healthcare system. My father's views should be taken with a grain of salt, for a few important reasons. For one, Steve's way of thinking reflect only his experience, which may or may not be relatable to you;

people's reactions to cancer can be widely different. There is nothing wrong with that. For another, there's a huge time difference: Steve passed away in 2003, so this story takes place between the years 2000–2003. There is a time lapse of over twenty years between Steve's death and the present day. Much has changed since then.

Nowadays, technology has brought us Netflix, self-driving cars, tablets, gene editing, robot agility, drones, and the iPhone. And it has also changed healthcare. Online appointments, for instance, were not a thing back in my father's day. The medical field has also seen massive breakthroughs helped or brought about by technological innovations, including the Human Genome Project, targeted cancer therapies, drug therapies that extend HIV survival, the HPV vaccine, robotic surgery, and bionic limbs, among others. With regards to cancer, too, there have been great advances and many new findings, especially since 2020—both in the treatment of cancer as a whole and in the treatment of colorectal cancer in particular.

Today, Stage IV colon cancer has a relative five-year survival rate of about 14%. This means that about 14% of people with stage IV colon cancer are likely to still be alive five years after they are diagnosed. Advances in areas such as biomedical technology and stem cell research have opened doors to many new fields in the medical industry and provided hope to millions of sufferers. There are now so many different ways to treat colorectal cancer – albeit not completely cure it – including radiation therapy, chemotherapy, immunotherapy, targeted therapy, hormone therapy, stem cell transplant, and precision medicine.

But while many things have changed since Steve battled the disease, others have not. Perhaps your experiences with the health system have been very different than my father's, or perhaps you have not spent much time in a healthcare setting. If so, you may find some of these stories eye-opening. Then again, if you are affected by a chronic disease or have had to spend a lot of time in hospitals or around medical professionals, you may find a lot of it relatable, even in this day and age. If that is the case, I hope, at the very least, that my father's story will show you that you are not alone.

Steve Grove:

There is a special code in the medical profession you'll have to learn to decipher. "You're going to feel a slight discomfort." Now, come on. I know that this means it's going to hurt like hell. I just laugh now when they say this. Or else they tell you, "You're going to feel a pinch." A pinch?! I think all doctors and nurses should have to spend three nights in a hospital and be required to go through the things that they prescribe to their patients. I often wonder if any of them have experienced any of the treatments they administer daily. I just want the colon doctors (GI doctors) to drink some of that "cleansing" fluid that they prescribe and then see if they ever refer to the process again as a "gentle cleansing." I am sure that they would approach those colonoscopies differently if they all had to have one done to them in medical school. That should be their final exam. I hear that people who draw blood will often practice on each other, so why shouldn't colon, kidney, stomach, or heart doctors be required to do the same? How can you possibly know what someone is going through if you have never experienced it?

I also think, more importantly, that before you can work for a health insurance company, you should be required to experience several injuries, diseases, and recoveries like those you have to rule on (I can hear many of you cheering now!). My surgeon told me that the insurance company would only cover a certain number of nights in the hospital. I didn't mind, as I was feeling better and was ready to go home; but I did wonder what happens to people who are not ready to go home. So, there should be a new law that, before you can work for a health insurance company, you have to have had some type of surgery or disease. This would make you more caring when you administer the treatment.

Josh Grove:

You're probably sitting there and wondering what state of mind my father may have been in as he wrote this. You may even be laughing at some of his comments. Just keep in mind the bigger picture of how he dealt with tough situations, from getting a colonoscopy or trying to get an appointment with a doctor. For my mother and me, watching someone so close to us suffering was not easy, but we could see that my father was trying to see the humor in the situation and remained, on the whole, optimistic. There are many things you can gain from going through tough situations like this, things that can shape who you become as a person. There can be a new positivity that takes root inside you when you are dealing with cancer—in a way, you have to cultivate this in order to carry on. In the end, every experience can shape who you are and lead to growth, positive or negative.

Re-encountering my father through his writing all these years later is a good example of this. Though some of it was painful for me to read, it was also an educational experience. It opened my eyes to aspects of my father's ordeal I might not have considered. I had, of course, visited my father in the hospital at the time. But as a child, I had not given much thought to the complexities that lay behind medical appointments and treatments, or to the healthcare system as a whole. My experience with hospitals is very different from my father's, and yours may be as well; a discussion on the merits and failings of our health system is not the point of this chapter, nor is it what you should necessarily take from it. But whether you agree with Steve's views or not, I encourage you to use every situation you encounter, every hurdle that life puts in your path, as an opportunity to acquire knowledge and insights. See it as a chance to grow as a person.

Many years after my father's passing, I realized that the suffering my family and I went through was, in some ways, a catalyst for my personal growth: my father's journey taught me so much about optimism, resilience and empathy for others. It has pushed me to get involved in charity work, and it has made me want to become better at asking for help. It has taught me patience. I won't sit here and tell you that I'm perfect or that I'm great at all of these things. I will tell you that I work at them every day. There are times when a situation does not go my way, or I am unable to solve a problem, and I get frustrated. Then I stop and realize that it's simply a learning experience. Many people have described my father as someone with a stubborn yet go-getter-type mentality, so I think he was similar to me in that way. That doesn't mean Steve didn't stumble along the way—at the end of the day, everyone progresses in their own way. But he learned from his mistakes as he stumbled. That's the key.

On an important side note, to those who have dealt with family members who have been affected by colon cancer, I highly recommend going to see your GI doctor and asking about a colonoscopy. As I grew older it became increasingly clear to me how important keeping your body and your colon healthy was. Whether the result of your colonoscopy is positive or negative, it is always better to know, so you can begin treating the issue. Postponing such a procedure could have serious and lasting consequences.

Again, I want to reiterate that there is a tremendous learning curve as you grow as a person. What I've learned is to never shy away from a difficult situation, but see it simply as a chance to get better. The more mistakes you make, the more you learn. Sometimes you may have to take two steps back to take one step forward. But there is no doubt that, by overcoming these challenging situations, you will, eventually, grow.

Steve Grove:

The hospital stay is horrible. People will wake you up just to see if you are sleeping. They take vital signs all day long, take blood when you can't even open your eyes, and there is not any resting that goes on in the evening in a hospital. Plus, remember that every minute of every hour of every day is the same for you... All you can think is, "Let me out of this place!" You really won't rest until you are home and able to get back into some type of routine.

They also have you share a room with someone else. At times, you even share a bathroom. So, you are paired with someone you don't know, at a time when you are both ill. I was quite lucky to have my own room, and that seemed to be a bit of luxury in the hospital, to have a private room. I have a friend who is high up at the hospital and called him ahead of time and asked him to reserve a room for me. Why not? For what you are paying per night in a hospital, shouldn't you have your own room? How do you share a room with someone else? They want to sleep while you are awake, you are sleeping while they want to visit with friends or family, and the problems go on and on. I won't even mention having to share a bathroom in the condition you are in...

Our medical system is broken. There are some major problems in the nurse-to-patient ratio and in the way they allocate nurses. I was afraid of that as I entered the surgery part of my treatment. My biggest worry was not having help when I needed it. I had made a call to the hospital before my admission and inquired about private duty nurses.

I had private duty nurses while I was in the hospital for the entire time. This was terribly expensive. I can't even begin to calculate the total, but for six days, when not even all the shifts were covered, we had to pay almost $4,000 in total. This was on top of my medical insurance paying for my time in the hospital...

We have reached disaster mode in our health system. I was on the sixth floor at Yale New Haven Hospital—one of the finest hospitals in the world, associated with one of the best medical schools in the world. How could I possibly go wrong? And yet. There are simply no nurses. Yale New Haven Hospital has 250 full-time nurse positions to fill. Can you imagine a huge place like that needing 250 staff members and nothing being done about it? How can ONE nurse take care of 8 to 11 sick people during an eight-hour shift that includes their breaks? How can they possibly care for us when we are sick while they are running around the other rooms? I was terribly fortunate to have some family and friends give me the money to pay for private-duty nursing. There would have been no other way. But this is the reason I did so well.

Josh Grove:

My father always tried to look at life from a glass-half-full perspective. It's clear that the situation into which he was thrown was far from perfect, yet he knew that he could not give up on himself or his family. He had to roll with the punches and find a way to get the care he needed. Luckily, Steve was not a person who would just dwell on the problems; he would always take action. So he fought back; he advocated for his own well-being. In this case, he insisted on having a private room, understanding that getting good care during his recovery could make a world of difference (while acknowledging also that this was a luxury). He knew that in times of crisis, every small comfort counts. He knew good care was crucial in his recovery. Remember, his number one priority was to beat cancer. As I read this, I remembered his mantra, which perfectly embodies his spirit of resilience: "It's not how hard you get hit; it's how quickly you can get back up and hit back."

Even though 20 years have passed since my father told me this, it still resonates with me today. Throughout our lives, we encounter a multitude of problems and challenges that we sometimes find hard to overcome; this struggle is an inherent part of the human experience. These challenges test our patience and tenacity. I have gone through some difficult times myself – my father's passing was one of those – and I understand how hard it is to get up when you've been knocked down. But it's important to try. I told myself, "If my father was able to get up and keep fighting even while being in extreme pain and undergoing chemotherapy, then so can I." It is amazing how much you can strengthen yourself with the right mindset.

Yet here's the thing: you have to believe in yourself in order to fight back. To overcome a problem, you have to trust that you can do it. Standing up and demanding change requires self-assuredness. From where I am sitting, there is no difference between not giving up in a tough situation and not giving up on yourself. My father's unwavering determination and belief in himself were key in how he dealt with the difficult situation he had found himself in: he decided to not only keep fighting cancer, but push himself to write a book about it! In this book, he would share his experiences with diagnosis, treatment, and recovery, highlight some of the hardships he encountered during this difficult journey, and also suggest solutions for fixing them. After all, as Steve was fond of saying, something good can always come out of something bad.

Steve Grove:

Who is to blame? Where did the problem start? I am sure it started with the insurance companies. Now, I am in business. I believe in jobs and business, and I understand the opportunity. But here's my take. The CEOs and top management of these companies don't need so much. That's the short and long of it. I heard recently that a CEO of an internet company had rented a ski house in Aspen for $400,000 during the week of Christmas for his family and friends. The stock is down 2,000%, and all I can say is, how dare he? Who do these people think they are, telling the healthcare system that they need managed care, when they haven't made any sacrifices themselves? This forces the hospitals to cut back, while it requires more nurses; people have to work harder, and often they leave the field. On top of that, no new nurses are coming into the field. The *system is broken, and someone better try to fix it. How can you possibly allow things to deteriorate to this level? How can any insurer allow a hospital to provide nursing care to their patients when the ratios are more than five patients to one nurse at all times? How can a nurse take care of more than that? This is the most ridiculous situation I have ever seen. Enough is enough.*

And this isn't new either. I was hospitalized with pancreatitis in March 1998. I can remember being at Yale New Haven Hospital for seven long days and constantly leaning on the call button for help. I needed changing, new sheets, medication, help to go to the bathroom, and so on. It took me three hours to get help one night to go to the bathroom. Can you imagine? THREE HOURS! Have you ever had to hold it in that long with nothing else to think about? I will never forget that I then tried to get out of bed myself and fell and wrenched my left shoulder. Yes, I got out myself and then hurt myself. The title of my book at that time was going to be "You Will Die at Shift Change." They have this "report" that all nurses do from one shift to another. It often lasts an hour and is done three to four times a day. On top of this, there aren't enough nurses. This has got to change.

Josh Grove:

What stands out to me about these passages is my father's determination to speak out against the unfairness he encountered. Steve didn't let adversity silence him; he used his voice to shed light on the problems he faced. He believed that truthfulness was key when highlighting the problems he identified within the medical system. Don't forget that his wish was to get this book published; he wanted to create a wave of change. In retrospect, his experience serves as a reminder that even in difficult situations, there are ways to make things better. While the medical system may still have its issues, my father's story teaches us that we have the power to stand up and make a difference, both for ourselves and for others facing similar challenges. And one of the ways in which we can do this is by sharing our stories with others. My father's attitude to being affected by cancer strengthened my resolve to try and get up faster and always fight back; and it also made me determined to finish the book he never did, so that others could learn from his experiences.

Steve Grove:

We need a change. Some suggestions to help this change is to force all hospital executives and insurance company executives to work with just one administrative assistant per several executives. Let's see what happens when they all want their lunch or dry cleaning at the same time. Let's see what happens when they all need their golf reservation made at the same time. I also suggest that all patients and customers of hospitals and insurance companies be allowed to set and vote on the expense accounts of the top executives. Let us determine what their spending is and how much of the customer's money goes to paying them. Are you telling me that there isn't any belt-tightening that can be done? I would love to get my hands on a few belts, and see how hard I can pull them. Again, I am not being cynical; I am trying to remain realistic. Stop asking us to accept the problems that aren't being addressed. We are being asked to share in the problems, but not to help provide the solutions.

At a small hospital here in Connecticut – Griffin Hospital in Derby – they have created a breast cancer center. I was interested and inquired what that was all about. What they explained was that a diagnosis of breast cancer means a ton of doctors, tests, results, visits, and coordination. They hired several people whose sole job was to coordinate all those issues. "What a wonderful idea!" I thought. It would be so nice if someone could have helped me with everything I had to deal with. Having someone by my side throughout this scary time would have been nice—someone to make the appointments, fight with the scheduling people about the times and dates of treatments, and so on... Why don't we make that happen?

Josh Grove:

A lot of this chapter deals with Steve's understandable frustration with his experiences in the hospital. In a way, though, this may be giving you the wrong idea about him. See, Steve was more than just a complainer; he was a doer. He didn't just point out the issues; he rolled up his sleeves and proposed real solutions. From where I'm standing, his suggestion to empower patients and customers to shape executives' expense accounts is a step towards true accountability. It's a reminder that we, as individuals, have a voice and can make a difference. His message rings loud and clear to me, so

144

many years later: we don't have to accept the problems that we see around us; we can and should be part of the solution. My father's unwavering determination to remain realistic and put forth suggestions to fix the issues he found himself confronted with serves as an inspiration, a testament to the power of one person's voice to spark change. I wish he were here today to see the improvements that have been made in healthcare, thanks in part to voices like his advocating for reform. His determination and courage continue to inspire me to this day.

Steve Grove:

Remember to fight for yourself. I know I have said this a lot in this book, but it's important. One of the problems you'll find in a teaching hospital is that there are so many doctors to talk to. Most of them are attending, residents, interns, and other fancy names. I still can't figure out who does what. I do know that they give different directions, think about things differently, like to look a lot, and mostly come in and out of your room all day long. Sometimes, it can be overwhelming. Various teams, groups, and individuals will come in and out. Sometimes they don't look at you like a human being; you are "Room 505/gallbladder." Don't let them do that to you. Remember that this may be a job for them, but it is your life.

Josh Grove:

Personal responsibility was one of my father's tenets, and something I identify strongly with as well. In his dealings with doctors and hospitals, Steve didn't just talk about reform from above. He didn't just put the onus on executives and politicians. He also believed that you have to roll with the punches, and that, in an imperfect system, each and every one of us should become our own advocates.

Steve Grove:

You are going to have to advocate for yourself. You can't imagine what system you are about to go into. Don't be afraid to ask about the doctors who are going to treat you. Ask them about their feelings on their success rates and whether they feel they can help you. Make sure they care about you. If you don't feel comfortable with them, chances are you won't be happy. We are fortunate, as we have a long-standing relationship with our physicians through my involvement in the community. Not everyone is so lucky, but ask

145

about your doctors. You know you would do the same when you are looking for an attorney, an accountant, or a place from which you can buy a car... So why would you do any less when you are sick?

Josh Grove:

When I think about the advice my father tried to give others battling with the same disease as him, it's a real eye-opener. He basically said, "Look out for yourself when you're dealing with the healthcare system because it's a wild ride." He wanted each person to take responsibility, to the best of their abilities, for their treatment, not simply leave it up to others. Indeed, he talks about this many times in his writing; it's clear this was something that he felt very strongly about.

Steve Grove:

Again, you will have to advocate for yourself. I had to pay attention to everything that was going on before and after surgery. It's up to you to schedule tests, ask questions, and keep people aware of the next step. One night in the hospital, before I was ready to leave, one of my nurses ordered me a full dinner. I knew I was still restricted to clear liquids, so I declined the meal and asked for more delicious hospital Jell-O (this has a half-life of one hundred years). I had to pay attention to when I was getting medication and when I needed it. I had to watch and ask questions about all the next steps. You must monitor the process and be aware of the next steps.

At times, during this process, I needed to talk to my doctors after 5:00 PM and on weekends. You'll find that pain and issues don't ever occur between 9:00 and 2:00, and 1:00 and 5:00 on Mondays, Tuesdays, Thursdays, and alternating Fridays (remember, physicians are off on Wednesdays and every other Friday). I am only kidding here, but my doctors did have to talk to me at times after hours. You're going to get the covering physician every once in a while, who needs to hear the whole story from top to bottom to help you. I know that there was more than one occasion when I had to call my doctors at home and beg them for some relief in one way or another. You may not feel as close to the covering doctor as you do to your own. I know that I only want to talk about my most intimate bodily functions with those I trust and like. Somehow, other doctors just never cut it. Don't feel bad about that, and don't worry about the covering physician. There may be times when you can go ahead and just wait until your doctor is back on duty; sometimes the effort of telling the whole story just isn't worth it.

Josh Grove:

I want to take the concept of advocacy that Steve suggests one step further. Think beyond advocating for yourself. Think also about advocating for others who are not in a position to do so. Do you have a friend or family member suffering from cancer – or some other condition – who is struggling to make themselves heard or who is not having their needs met? Perhaps you can become an advocate for them. Speak up on their behalf if you know they are unable to. In my case, being involved in charity work, along with raising money for cancer research makes me feel like I am advocating for my father, who is no longer here to advocate for himself.

Now, being an advocate doesn't necessarily have to take one specific shape. There are many ways you can help a loved one when they are battling cancer, whether that is being there for them every step of the way, making appointments, talking with doctors, offering to help with chores, visiting them in the hospital, or simply being someone they can talk to on the phone and confide in. It does not matter how you choose to exert your energy; just try to have a positive impact on the lives of people around you. You are never going to be able to fix everyone's problems, but you can try to lessen the burden.

Make sure you are in the right state of mind for this. Do not do this if you are feeling fragile; do not try to give more than you have to give at any given moment. First, focus on your happiness, and then worry about everyone else's. But if you are in a good place, take a minute to think about who in your life could use a hand. Reach out to that person. You will be amazed how much of a difference you can make in someone's life. And if you don't have someone in your life who needs you to speak up for them, you can always be an advocate for change by supporting a cause you believe in and can stand behind. Remember what we talked about previously: find your *why*, and you will discover what advocacy can mean for you.

Previously, I have mentioned my work with sponsoring events in college or working at various charity events. One of my goals when I decided to write about my father's story was to raise awareness about current day colon cancer research and encourage people to donate or get involved. Cancer is still all around us. The American Cancer Society has reported that an estimated 1,372,910 new cases of cancer were diagnosed in the United States in 2005, a year in which over 540,000 people died from cancer. In 2018, an estimated 1,735,350 new cases of cancer were diagnosed in the United States and over 609,000 people died from the disease. When it comes to the specific type of cancer Steve suffered from, the ACS statistics tell us that, in 2020, approximately 147,950 individuals were diagnosed with colorectal cancer and 53,200 died from the disease, with 104,610 cases of colon cancer and 43,340 cases of rectal cancer. Of these, 17,930 cases and 3,640 deaths were of individuals aged younger than fifty years. So, unfortunately, chances are cancer will touch your life in one way or another, whether it's affecting a close friend, a distant relative, or a friend of a friend of a coworker.

Colorectal cancer is the second most common killer. Research on this particular type of cancer has always been quite slow because of the severity and complexity of the disease. However, over the last decade or so, there have been several promising discoveries that truly make a difference in the lives of people affected by colon cancer. One doctor, Helen Chen, MD, has described this era as a particularly hopeful period for colon cancer sufferers: *"This is a very exciting moment in the treatment of colorectal cancer. For a long time, we just weren't able to do much in terms of making a real difference in a patient's care. But now we have new medications that really show improvement in the survival of people with the disease."*[1]

My father's battle with cancer was a huge part of my childhood and affected my entire family. In many ways, it hit me harder than I could understand at the time. As time went on, I tried to view my experiences with it in a positive light and use them to spur myself into action. I surrounded myself with friends who also embraced charity work and sponsored events. I wanted to continue to increase efforts to raise money for cancer research. There were always uphill challenges and battles to climb. It takes a great deal of patience and resilience to not give up when faced with planning hiccups or when not meeting donation goals. But knowing that your efforts and energy are going towards a great cause helps uplift you spiritually and keep you going.

---

[1] (Chen, WebMD)

Knowing that the money you helped raise is allowing doctors to continue to help cancer patients and scientists to continue searching for a cure is incredibly rewarding. Each new discovery or promising new treatment in the medical field feels like a personal win.

Admittedly, there is no perfect cure out there for colorectal cancer yet. But your donations and efforts are not going to waste. New discoveries are being made every day, and researchers believe that many of these new discoveries are a cause for real hope. The two main drugs that were used in treating colon cancer from the 1960s until recently were Adrucil and Wellcovorin. Over the last twenty years, medical researchers continued to work towards developing treatments, and many clinical trials were carried out to test the efficacy of the newly developed drugs. This paid off. In 2019 two new colorectal cancer drugs were approved: Avastin and Erbitux. Both of these drugs have opened the floodgates to the development of new treatments that simply had not been an option before, and which may improve the quality of life of cancer sufferers.

When people talk about cancer, they often talk about survival rates. If you are affected by cancer or have a loved one who is, I want you to think about that word: survival. This is defined in the Oxford Languages Dictionary as, "continuing to live or exist, typically in spite of an ordeal or difficult circumstances." It doesn't necessarily describe *how* you are living. But what if your quality of life was able to improve so that you were not merely surviving? Wouldn't you jump at that opportunity? Of course you would. This is why it's important to continue raising money for research, even if a definite cure for cancer may not be on the immediate horizon.

Chapter 13: Never Give Up

Steve Grove:

Chemotherapy used to be done over a few days in the hospital. Colonoscopies used to be two- to three-day procedures; you are now in and out of the hospital in four hours, including recovery—not quite a "drive-through" service, but almost. Recovery, too, was mostly done in the hospital. Now, chances are you'll do a lot more recuperating at home than you used to some twenty years ago.

Healing at home will not be pleasant for your family. Remember that they are used to seeing you up and around. They are used to you helping with the chores, doing the dishes, going to work, and mowing the lawn. They aren't used to you sitting around and sleeping a little extra. They aren't used to you being weak, so understand a bit of what they are going through. Try not to gross out your family too much. I know that sounds harsh, but although you may not mind all the medical stuff going on, they won't be used to it. My son made the worst face of "Gross, gross, gross!" when I showed him my scar while I was still in the hospital. He had said he wanted to see it, but I realized after that there was no need for anyone to look at it.

Josh Grove:

My father was very good at hiding his emotions. At this stage in his chemotherapy – while he was mostly out of the hospital and spending time recovering at home – he felt that hiding his true feelings about the treatments he was undergoing was important. It was necessary to keep the people around him strong. He knew how high the mountain that he was climbing was but, if he ever found the journey daunting, he never let his family know how he felt about it. If you have any loved ones who have been affected by cancer, then you may be able to relate to this. I watched my father struggle, while all the while he tried to maintain a calm, cool, and collected attitude so he wouldn't scare me. It was his way of responding to the stress he was under.

A lot of people have described Steve as funny, upbeat, cheerful. And if you are perceived to be something, you become it (remember what we discussed before: *perception is reality*). At the end of the day, a person's character and personality becomes solidified in other people's minds. So it can be hard to express a different side of yourself. My father never shared his preoccupations, his suffering, his burdens. Possibly, he wanted to remain unchanged; he wanted people to remember him as they had known him. Possibly, he felt he had a duty to protect his family. Whatever you are going through in your personal life, don't do this.

I, too, have had times in my life when I encountered obstacles that felt unsurmountable, challenges that felt impossible to face. In my own journey, I've found that this is precisely when the "phone a friend" option becomes invaluable. Having a circle of close friends and family to lean on during tough times can make such a difference. Identifying those who can serve as empathetic sounding boards without judgment is equally crucial. Trust the people you surround yourself with. They are around you for a reason. Whether it's your family, friends, or spiritual leaders (or doctors, when it comes to your health) having them by your side will be key in your ability to overcome the challenge.

Admitting that you need help is the first step. I can't imagine many people would disagree with this in theory, but for a great number of people, it is easier said than done. This is something I have personally struggled with, as well. I have always been wary of asking for help and found it hard to admit I might be unable to deal with something. I know I get my stubbornness from my father. Sometimes you feel a need to prove you can do it alone or that you don't need anyone's advice but your own. But after many years of wrestling with the concept, I realized that it is better to keep an open mind to other people's advice rather than getting stuck. Learning to swallow my pride has been a crucial step in my individual growth. My willingness to seek help from others is something I've undergone a complete 180-degree shift in. At the end of the day, life is a journey, and we are all on board for the ride. There may be moments when we find ourselves at a crossroads or facing uncertain paths. And just as seasoned travelers know the wisdom of seeking local guidance when navigating foreign lands, we must also recognize the invaluable assistance that others can provide on our personal odysseys. In the grand voyage of life, seeking help from fellow travelers can be the compass that leads us to smoother seas.

Steve Grove:

The first thing the hospital tells me is that they only allow three nursing agencies into the hospital to provide private duty nurses. They gave me three agency names as recommendations to find private duty care. Have you ever opened up the phone book and looked under health or nursing care? You would be amazed! With dozens and dozens of agencies to choose from, the hospital only allows three to provide these caregivers. Can you get any more ridiculous? They should be falling all over these agencies and getting them signed up by the dozens. One of the agencies just laughed when I asked about getting some nurses for a few weeks. They had none available for months and had not had any available in the prior few months. I had to laugh, too. Why then, would the hospital give out its name? The second agency had maybe one person for a few shifts and even that would be questionable. They told me they would search and call me back; they would "see what they could do." I laughed again, looking for the candid camera at this point. Are you starting to get the picture? This system is just a joke. Why is the hospital giving out these names when these organizations are useless? There must have been some financial arrangement between the particular agencies and the hospital.

The third agency seemed to be a home run, as this nice coordinator said she could get me care for most of the shifts, from the day I got out of surgery until I went home. They were a great agency and they have been around for about eighty years, as far as I could tell. They sent Sarah to be my day nurse, who was there from 7:00 AM to 3:00 PM for four of the days. She was wonderful and provided more than care. She was encouraging, funny, and helped me get better. This is why you need good nursing care. It isn't just about having some medicine administered. It is about getting well and having someone there who cares and who helps get your mind off your troubles. She helped me line up all the various shifts for private care and checked carefully on all aspects of me. When one of the private nurses called out for a few shifts, she went around the hospital asking nurses who also worked for this agency if they were available. I was so thankful and knew that my recuperation was due in large part to her and her assistance.

They sent me Connie for a few evening shifts. I awoke when she arrived the first night and I thought Florence Nightingale had appeared. Connie is seventy years old and wears a nurse's dress, stockings, and a hat. She looked like she had stepped out of a 1950s movie and treated me like she was June Cleaver. She was right there, took good care of me and I felt so comfortable having her there for the evening. The only drawback to Connie, was... well, let me put this lightly. Each of the various nurses you'll meet have their own ways about them: one will take blood pressure a certain way, some will draw blood in a certain way, and so on. Connie was great, except she didn't believe in these new-fangled thermometers. They used to take your temperature in your ear, mouth, or under the arm... so a few times each evening, well, you can guess the rest here. She was gentle, yet accurate. I only wish she had been able to be there every evening. Unfortunately, she had a death in her family and had to be out of town for a week or so. She was wonderful!

The rest of the private duty nurses I had were more or less memorable and helpful, but it was the fact that you had someone right there when you needed something that made a difference. When it was time for vitals, medications, or a trip to the bathroom, you had the help you needed. There was no leaning on the buzzer and praying that someone would get there in under three hours.

Good nursing care will be a life-saver in terms of your whole attitude. If you are treated and taken care of, you will feel better quicker. I know that having my sheets changed, getting cleaned, and having various tubes taken out when it was time to do so helped me recover quickly. There were people on the floor who would wait hours for things to happen. I know from my 1998 experience that this just slowed things down terribly. When you ask for help, you need to have that help ready and present. This may be a narrow view of the world, coming from a patient's standpoint, but all these institutions are competing for my business, so why shouldn't they be customer-friendly? Why should they not practice all the various things they advertise in all their booklets? If you have a right to good care, you should get it.

Josh Grove:

Reflecting on Steve's experiences and the valuable lessons he shared, it's abundantly clear that two fundamental principles shaped his journey: persistence and gratitude. He understood that achieving his goals required adaptability, a willingness to ask the right questions, and a genuine appreciation for those who extended their help. These qualities weren't just a means to an end; they were cornerstones of his approach to life.

Let's take the first: gratitude. Think back to moments in your life when you were going through a difficult time and had to dig deep in order to be able to express gratitude to those who were helping you. Did that make the situation better? Whether you are dealing with financial, emotional, or practical challenges, or even battling a formidable opponent like cancer, often, it's that very expression of thanks that can become the key to solving the puzzle before you. Did you find a lesson there you can take with you?

My father certainly did. By way of illustration, I wanted to share the following short paragraph, which I found both amusing and illuminating; Steve wrote it before going in for one of the many procedures he underwent during his treatment:

Steve Grove:

I met with my banker also before going in for surgery. It was somewhat like talking to the rabbi. "I am going to be out for a while. I haven't felt well in months, and I need some breathing space." He said, "Okay, let's do it." I could not believe how good he was to me. I suppose I expected the worst, as I prepared for some time out and knew that my banker was very important in the life of my business and my personal survival. Don't forget your banker!

Josh Grove:

The second quality I deeply admire in how my father handled this difficult situation was persistence. When it came to his recovery, thankfully, my father did admit he needed help and he went out of his way to ask for it, despite the hurdles that the healthcare system threw at him. It must have taken a lot of courage and determination to do that; I have said before that my father was an extremely self-sufficient person who hated burdening others with his problems. But sometimes simply asking for help is not enough. We might get turned down or be unable to find the right person; there might be practical, financial, or bureaucratic problems that prevent us from getting the help we need. It takes persistence to carry on seeking.

Steve demonstrates this. The first nursing care agency didn't pan out; the second either; but the third did. He was relentless in his efforts and willing to swallow his pride to get what he needed at that time. He was aware that getting help might increase his chances of a good recovery and improve his prognosis. Indeed, he writes earlier that competent help from his nurses is the very reason he recovered so quickly after surgery; he calls it a "life-saver." He knew that battling his cancer head on would be a long and daunting journey, but it was the only path to survival, so he continued to fight.

Many people tend to choose the easy way out or go out of their way to avoid difficult situations, confrontations, or challenges. Some simply don't want to deal with them or feel that it will be a losing battle anyway, so fighting is not worth the effort. For my family, having dealt with my father's disease for the better half of my childhood, you could say challenge and adversity was part of our lives. My mother and I knew it would be an uphill battle, potentially even an unwinnable one. However, we did not give up; we knew that we had to stay positive and keep going. My quest to put the pieces of this story together required a similar determination and resilience. It took a lot of years to talk to everyone who knew Steve, to go through his writings, and respond to each one of them with my personal take-aways, but I knew I had to persevere and finish this book. You see, this mentality is something my father instilled in me from a young age, way before his battle with cancer would commence.

As any good parent would, Steve tried to pass down to me any knowledge and advice that he felt was important, in ways that I could understand. My father was fond of sayings and aphorisms, and there are quite a few of his that appear throughout this book. The one I remember the most is a piece of simple advice that came from a man we both admired, Jim Valvano. For those not familiar with the name, Jim Valvano – or Jimmy V – was an American college basketball player, coach, and broadcaster who was active from the '60s to the early '90s. During his time as a coach at North Carolina State University, he won the 1983 Division 1 Men's College Basketball

National Championship. He became one of the biggest sports icons in the college community and was known for having a gritty coaching style and expecting the best from his players. Just like Steve, Jim battled with cancer in the later years of his life. In June 1992, he was diagnosed with metastatic adenocarcinoma, a type of glandular cancer that can spread to the bones.

My father was very fond of Jimmy V and introduced me to him at a young age. As I grew up learning more about the sports world, I became a fan of his as well. In March 1993, Jimmy V gave one of the most iconic speeches in sports history at the famous ESPY Awards—a yearly awards ceremony hosted by ESPN to celebrate athletic performance and sports-related achievements. The awards celebrate not only athletes' performance on the field, but also off it, focusing also on the impact athletes have had on their communities. In this famous speech, Jimmy talks about how important it is to know where you are and where you are going in life. He goes on to say that you must have a dream, a goal in life, and you have to be willing to work for it. This was an idea that greatly appealed to Steve, even before he got sick; from a young man, he had always pushed himself to work hard in order to make his dreams come true.

At the ceremony, Jimmy V received the Arthur Ashe Courage and Humanitarian Award, and he announced the creation of The V Foundation for Cancer Research, an organization dedicated to finding a cure for cancer. Today, the V Foundation has awarded more than $175 million in cancer research grants nationwide. The tenet upon which he founded the foundation was "*Don't give up... Don't ever give up.*" This line hit home for my dad both personally and as a sports fan. Even though he heard it well before he was diagnosed, it became one of his mantras, and it is something that has stuck with me throughout the years. I may not have understood it fully as a child, but with time, I started to understand the value of perseverance, as sports became more and more a part of my life.

Every sports fan knows that sports is not just about competition; it is also about the story. There is a lot of emotion involved. We are sad when our team loses, and we are ecstatic when they win. Of course, a great triumph against the odds is always exciting, but what I have learned over the years is that a great defeat can be inspiring, too. We have all witnessed those moments where our team loses, yet everyone claps for them anyway because they have given it their all and fought bravely to the end. If there is one single thing that I want you to get out of this book, it is to never give up on yourself; never stop trying. Even when it is hard, keep fighting—just like Jimmy V did, and just like my father did. They both battled cancer to the very end. Neither came out on top, but both will be remembered for never giving up. And that certainly deserves a clap.

Chapter 14: Life Goes On

Josh Grove:

The next part of the story will reveal the outcome of Steven Grove's life. My father spent much of his last few years in doctor's offices. He tried to make the most out of every situation and did his best to cope, sometimes through humor. He talks earlier about his hope to add more advice for cancer sufferers as his healing progresses. Unfortunately, he never got that opportunity. If it's not clear enough by now, Steve did not survive cancer. So he never got to finish his book. I thought, "I could pick up where he left off. I could fill in the blanks, complete the full picture." This is the main reason why I wanted our writing to be intertwined. This dialog across the years would give readers what Steve's journal alone couldn't: the whole story, from his past up to the present day.

When a loved one dies, people will often tell you that "life goes on." How many times have you heard that phrase? I'm sure you've come across it in songs, movies, TV shows, poems, and novels, whether verbatim, or different variations on the cliché. But when you stop and actually think about it, all of the set phrases that talk about "moving on" or "life carrying on" carry more profound meanings than obvious at first glance. This is not something you will want to accept, especially when you are in pain, and people will not stop repeating those expressions. In the midst of your own grief, they will seem like hollow platitudes. In time, however, you will find that what you were told is true: time passes, and you eventually come to terms with it. There are things you can do that can help you through the process. Therapy or grief counseling can be helpful. For me, writing this book was also one of them.

To give you some context, I am currently in my early 30s. I had decided to start this project a few years ago. It felt like the right time. Stories were something I always connected with and that had a deep impact on me, even as a child. So, I wanted to include here not only Steve's thoughts on the experiences he underwent during his battle with cancer, but also stories from people who knew him, who were keen to share their memories of him and talk about the impact he had had on their lives. Over the last few years, I was able to connect with various close friends and relatives of my father's. Throughout the rest of this chapter, I will share some stories and anecdotes from some of Steve's closest friends. These shed light on earlier parts of his life – before he was diagnosed – and on who he was as a person. As you read, continue to pause to think about your own life, and see how these stories may be relevant to you. I hope you will walk away with some take-aways you can apply in your own life.

One of the first people I spoke to was David Gordon, a lifelong friend of my father's, who also happens to be my godfather. He shared a treasure trove of humorous anecdotes with me that never fail to make me smile. To offer some context about David, he had known my mother first; their childhoods were intertwined due to their parents' deep-rooted friendship. David had the distinct privilege of working alongside both my mother and father in various capacities, notably through their involvement in United Synagogue Youth and their shared experiences at Camp Sequassen, a Boy Scout camp nestled in Connecticut.

David had mentioned to me several years back that he truly admired how my father navigated the challenges of surgeries and cancer rehabilitation. David talked a lot about how protective Steve was of his friends, emphasizing how Steve always assumed the role of a guardian. He told me a story about when they worked together at Camp Sequassen, where Steve was the Director of the camp and David was the Assistant Director of the ropes course. When Steve went to talk to David about his pay for the summer, he whispered, "Dave, don't tell anyone what you are making, but your pay for the summer is an extra 50 bucks more than everyone else." Even the smallest gesture to help a friend was important to him. It was Steve's way of showing his loyalty to David, thanking him for joining him, while extending a helping hand at the same time.

David told me that Steve had an exceptional ability to shift conversations about his battle with cancer toward Dave's own life, offering valuable guidance on cherishing every moment with his family. During one of David's visits to Steve in the hospital, Steve greeted him with a warm smile. When David inquired about Steve's well-being, Steve's response was both selfless and profound: "Don't worry about me; I'm fine. Worry about raising your children and taking good care of them. Cherish every moment you have with them." Dave told me this was typical of Steve; even as he faced his own mortality, Steve steadfastly avoided discussing his own situation or the inevitable outcome. He remained resolute in his belief that he could overcome the odds. Steve's focus was on sparing his friends from the burden of concern about his diagnosis or condition; his concern was always directed at his loved ones. David remembers Steve as a pillar of strength, not just for himself but for his entire family.

This resonates with my memories of him, as well. If he was hurting or in pain, he never showed it. I remember that he would worry more for me than he did about himself and his health. He gave me a sense of what selfless love and loyalty means from a very young age. Looking back on it now, he was always trying to maintain a facade, steadfastly concealing any signs of distress. He didn't want to focus on the pain; he only focused on beating cancer. My father was a true embodiment of Jimmy V's "Never give up" mentality, and he wished to impart this unwavering determination to his close friends and family. As I listened to David's numerous anecdotes about my father, I began to realize just how much my father's values aligned with mine.

An old friend of our family's, Linda Spivack, played a unique role in Steve's life. She not only developed a deep fondness for my father through their professional interactions but also shared a commonality with him: her son Jeff and I attended preschool together. As our parents grew closer, so did we; we soon became close friends. And while we drifted apart over time, this book has in a way brought us back together. Linda often shared with me the joy it brought my father to witness not only my growth but also that of her son. On one occasion, she said to me, "Josh, you were the joy of your father's life. You meant the absolute world to him. He did whatever it took to make sure you knew that and that you thought he was okay. He always tried to keep a tough exterior." She continued to speak about my father's unwavering loyalty and described how my mother stood by his side until the very end of his life.

As my father faced mounting challenges, Linda remained a constant presence, extending her help in various ways, from giving me rides home from school to ensuring I made it to sports practices. Linda and her husband George were always there to support us. Looking back on those times as an adult, I am immensely grateful for the countless acts of kindness shown by Linda, George, and their family. We have maintained a close connection with them, and both me and my mother treasure these lasting memories.

One of my father's oldest friends, Adam Kligfeld, graciously shared the impact my father had on his life. Their friendship began when Adam was in eighth grade, and Steve was in his early twenties. Adam recalled how my father had a keen interest in motivating him to participate in local organizations. Steve encouraged Adam to join youth groups in the area and consistently urged him to strive for excellence. He described my father as a determined and extremely persuasive individual, qualities that Adam greatly admired. Adam felt that Steve genuinely cared about making him feel welcome and involved. As I have detailed in various parts of this book, my father was a passionate and driven person, and Adam recognized these qualities in him early in their friendship.

Adam eventually became the National President of USY. For those unfamiliar with USY, it's a youth organization that brings young Jewish teenagers together to contribute to their local Jewish communities. It's an excellent way for high-schoolers to engage with a youth group beyond the classroom. My father's encouragement deeply influenced Adam and played a significant role in guiding him towards his path to becoming a Rabbi. Adam now resides in California, serving as a Rabbi in a well-known synagogue in the greater Los Angeles area.

After speaking with Adam, I could hear in his voice just how important my father had been to him and how much affection he had felt for him. He told me they used to play racquetball together and that they shared the same dry sense of humor. He mentioned he found comfort and guidance in their interactions. There was a period when they lost touch, he said, but in the early 2000s, when my father became ill, they reconnected. Adam visited him quite frequently in the hospital. In several of their final conversations, my father sought his rabbinical advice, just as Adam once sought my father's advice and guidance in his younger years. While my father asked Adam many questions, not necessarily seeking concrete answers but more interested in his opinion, Adam did his best to offer his outlook on life, just as my father had done for him many years earlier. Their friendship had come full circle.

Another close friend of Steve's was Dena Shulman (now Shulman-Green), who also got to know my father through USY. This happened while she was in high school, with my mother serving as the Connecticut Regional Director of USY and my father working as a staff member. At that time, Dena was just a member of the youth group. She looked up to him as an authority figure within the group, someone who exuded leadership qualities. Eventually, Dena transitioned to a staff member role within the youth group. When she described their relationship to me, she mentioned its various phases, highlighting how it evolved and transformed over time, much like any enduring friendship. When you've been friends since your teenage years and continue that connection into adulthood, you naturally witness different facets of each other.

To provide some insight into Dena, she worked at Yale New Haven Hospital, where she conducted research on various cancers and offered solace to individuals grappling with cancer and the prospect of mortality. She spoke about the close bond between Adam and Steve during their teenage and early adolescent years. She also emphasized that my father was Adam Kligfeld's most ardent supporter and close confidant. According to her, Steve derived immense satisfaction from his role as a mentor and felt invigorated by it. During our conversations, Dena and her husband, Eric Green, shared some insightful perspectives on my father. They both affirmed that Steve had a genuine affinity for the sense of community that came with being part of something larger than yourself. This is why he was so deeply involved in organizations like The Boy Scouts of America and United Synagogue Youth.

She talked about him at length. She said that, whenever a problem arose or a task needed attention, he never hesitated; he simply took action. She told me that he was a natural leader who thrived on assisting others and finding solutions. His perpetual smile and knack for finding humor in any situation brightened up any room he entered. He also loved keeping busy; he believed there was always something to do. He possessed a friendly, outgoing, and go-getter mindset, effortlessly connecting with people in his conversations and interactions. Building rapport with others brought him immense joy, and he enjoyed getting to know people better.

When Dena and I talked about my father, I felt that her words were genuine and heartfelt; I was also touched by them. She stressed several times that Steve's most significant achievement and proudest moments revolved around being a father to me. He had always felt a strong responsibility toward those around him and took immense pleasure in mentoring young people. Naturally, he aimed to guide me and aspired to be the ultimate role model and mentor for me. He didn't get to play that role for too long, and it is a loss I still feel deeply today. What lessons might I have learned under his tutelage that I never got to learn? What truths about myself and the world that I eventually arrived at on my own would I have gotten to sooner?

Eric, a local accountant in Hamden, got to know my father through their professional lives. He mentioned how proud my father was of owning his own business, S. Grove & Associates, in the late '90s and early '20s. Eric saw my dad as a coach and consultant in the local accounting industry. He said Steve knew everyone and often emphasized the importance of attending events, networking, and meeting new people. "You just never know who you're going to meet; anything can happen," Steve would tell Eric.

This brings us to the last part of this story, the ending, which shows how my father treated and interacted with people at the end of his life. Dena told me she went to see Steve about two or three weeks before he passed away. She noticed that Steve looked ill and weakened and said to him jokingly, "Steve, you don't look like yourself." He told her that he was okay and that she shouldn't worry. That was his attitude—never dwelling on his condition, always looking forward. She thought to herself that if he wasn't dwelling on it, then neither should she. But she left the facility with a heavy heart, feeling like their roles had reversed: she thought he would be sad, and she would have to cheer him up; instead she was sad, and he had tried to reassure her. She knew Steve's assurance that he was okay was intended to ease her worries and prevent her from feeling sorry for him. Unfortunately, she didn't realize that it would be the last time she'd have the chance to speak to him. Dena and Eric wrapped up our conversation by emphasizing my father's unwavering optimism. "He looked on the bright side of life," she said. In the midst of his battle with cancer, Steve had found peace, somehow. He didn't complain about life being unfair, begrudge others their health, or wish he could be in their shoes.

Rabbi X, a close friend of my father's who has chosen to remain anonymous, plays a significant role in his story. Their bond was profound; this person knew Steve better than most people. Hailing from Brooklyn, they assumed the role of Rabbi at Or Shalom Synagogue in Orange, Connecticut, at the age of 32. In the early 1980s, Or Shalom merged with another Orange synagogue to create a larger community. In 1983, a pivotal year, my father and this person embarked on a remarkable journey together. Their relationship was marked by collegiality, mutual appreciation, and trust. Their first encounter occurred when Steve applied for the Youth Leader position at the synagogue, a role he pursued tenaciously. He kept pestering their office about his application and followed up through frequent inquiries and follow-up calls. The role he sought was Youth Leader, and this title went beyond a mere job description; it entailed the important task of guiding young individuals and having a positive impact in their lives. When I spoke to this person, they recalled their initial interview at their Brooklyn residence, humorously noting that what they remember that there had been diapers scattered all around the apartment, and Steve had not commented on this—at that time, this person had recently become a parent.

After a few weeks, Steve secured the position. Not only did he embrace the challenge, but he also approached his job responsibilities with unwavering dedication. Creating a youth group was one of my father's passions. His innate spirituality and sense of purpose led him to see himself as a messenger uplifting others. His popularity within the community and among his peers bolstered his case. As he grew into his role, synagogue leadership began to grow wary of Steve's influence and the community's power he wielded. Nevertheless, Steve excelled in lobbying for all the right reasons. He relished building relationships, understanding people's desires, and always had the community's best interests at heart. This person told me: "There was always this intensity and passion with everything he did. He wasn't going to stop at a no. Whatever Steve wanted, he got." They believed that Steve's intensity might have stemmed from the loss of his sister. Being able to deal with such a tragedy and move on drove him to excel. Perhaps he felt he needed to accomplish what his sister now

164

couldn't; we will never know. From my perspective today, I can relate to this. Enduring such a traumatic event can affect you in profound, often unexpected, ways. Not all of them are negative. Steve's ability to channel that negative energy into something productive and positive left a lasting impact on many lives, even now, more than 40 years later. This person explained that Steve cultivated a dedicated following within the group, many of whom may still feel indebted to him today. He mentioned that not a few people would even say that Steve was the synagogue's greatest youth leader ever, as he not only established an exceptional youth group but also elevated the synagogue's profile in the international Jewish youth movement. Steve often took the group on retreats, persistently encouraging the rabbi to join them. He also became a surrogate older brother to teenagers in the community who were facing challenging times, offering them guidance and support.

Steve's time at Temple Or Shalom was a major highlight of his life, but as everything else, including life itself, it eventually came to an end. As he grew older, met my mother, and eventually had me, things naturally evolved. Their lives took different turns, and they ventured into new chapters. Starting a family was the next big adventure in Steve's life. As his family dynamic shifted, so did his connection with others, including Dena, in the ever-unfolding story of life. Of course, all relationships change in some way over time; it's about how you adapt and prioritize what's in front of you.

Now, let's dive into my dad's involvement with the Boy Scouts of America, where he made another close friend, John Petrillo. To set the scene, their scouting journey began in the late 1980s. Back in their early years, John and my dad crossed paths in elementary and middle school. John was a 4th grader while my dad was in 6th grade, but it wasn't until my dad reached 9th grade that they truly connected. The catalyst for their friendship? As they navigated through the challenges and adventures of scouting, their friendship flourished. Together, they embarked on thrilling journeys, including participating in multiple international jamborees. The World Boy Scout Jamboree, an event organized by the World Organization of the Scout Movement, brought together thousands of scouts from around the world, typically aged fourteen to seventeen. With a legacy spanning over a century, this organization has united young scouts across generations. John and Steve's friendship was cemented through their shared scouting adventures, creating a unique and lasting connection.

Over the years, their paths occasionally diverged, especially during their college years. However, after John completed his college journey, they rekindled their connection, spending memorable summers together. My father, who graduated from high school in 1981 and attended a local college while living at home, assumed a leadership role at Camp Sequassen. By 1986, he had risen to the position of youth director at the camp. In 1988, John also completed his college education, and shortly thereafter, he decided to follow my father's path. In 1992, Steve persuaded John to join him at the camp. The influence my father had on John through their shared scouting experiences was profound. Their summers leading groups of kids left an indelible mark on countless lives. John depicted my father as the kind of person who befriended everyone, genuinely cared about others, and took a keen interest in their well-being. Steve possessed an unmistakable charisma that drew people to him; he was, without a doubt, a larger-than-life figure. Through his involvement in scouting, youth organizations, various other groups, and his local accounting firm, Steve touched the lives of hundreds, if not thousands. As John aptly put it, "Steve's impact has probably spread all over the world." I was told that there were close to 600 people at his funeral, a testament to the countless lives he had touched. I had not counted attendance, but I can remember there being a line of people outside the funeral home, waiting to pay their respects. Although I did not know many of them, I was gifted with many stories about my father.

Although rooted in the scouts, John and Steve's connection ran deep, extending beyond this shared interest. In the early nineties in Connecticut, my dad became part of a local business called the Barter Network. This unique system allowed professionals to exchange their services for something else of value. While it primarily involved small businesses, some franchises also participated, and the organization still thrives today. Given that my father owned his own accounting firm, he could offer accounting services in exchange for various perks— memberships at racquetball courts, timeshares in destinations like Aruba or Vermont for skiing, or home improvements like framing and window treatments. However, Steve didn't stop at a fair trade; he always went the extra mile. His generosity knew no bounds. For instance, he'd take older boy scout leaders on weekend skiing trips to Vermont. Let's pause for a moment to contemplate one word: generosity. Being a generous person doesn't necessitate giving away thousands of dollars or countless hours to charities. It's about lending a hand to those less fortunate and assisting those around you without being asked. This word holds various meanings, as I'm sure you can appreciate. Regardless of your circumstances, take a moment to consider how you can help others and give back, much like my father and John did within the scouting community. John remained deeply involved in scouting as a professional and even rose to the position of Regional VP of Scouting in the Northeast Region in 2000.

I want to share one final story that illustrates how Steve's impact continues to resonate with John, even today. On Memorial Day weekend in 2003, my father invited John to visit Connecticut, knowing. John lived in the Atlanta area at the time. However, John and his wife, Maureen, had already planned to visit John's father in June, a few days after my dad's passing, and were uncertain if they could come earlier. Unfortunately, John didn't get to see my father one last time. Yet, to this day, John wears my father's old Boy Scouts dress shirts, as he remains actively involved in his local scouting organizations. While they couldn't connect before Steve's passing, two decades later, John still holds Steve's memory dear, while honoring and preserving his legacy.

The last friend of my fathers I spoke to is Paul Ryder, another of my father's friends from the scouting world. Paul's friendship with my father began in the late '70s. At that time, Paul was in his early teens. They met at Troop 604, the local Boy Scouts troop in Hamden, Connecticut, where Steve and my family lived. During this period, Steve held the position of senior patrol leader. Over the years, their friendship deepened, especially during the summers spent at Camp Sequassen, the same place where Steve formed a close bond with John Petrillo. From 1977 to 1981, both Steve and Paul assumed leadership roles in Troop 604. This was the period when they were closest. Steve achieved his Eagle Scout Award in 1979, and Paul earned his in 1982. The Eagle Scout Award stands as the highest achievement in the local scouting movement. As they later ventured into college life, their friendship naturally ebbed and flowed. They would spend summers and breaks in between semesters together, but for the most part, each had his own circle of friends.

Paul saw Steve as a role model. Steve told Paul that anyone in the group can be a leader. See, Paul aspired to be a leader in the group himself and learned a lot by watching how Steve conducted himself. Steve would help lead and organize big events and was always there for others. He was a prominent figure in the community, known as the person who could "make things happen." People looked up to him. Paul thought, "If he can do it, so can I." Later in life, Paul became a troop leader when his own children entered scouting, and he acknowledged Steve's enduring influence on him.

Paul described my father as a funny, light-hearted person on the whole, but he did feel that Steve was carrying the weight of the world on his shoulders. This is something I want to take a minute to talk about. It is something I have thought a lot about as I sat and wrote this book. After hearing many people's personal stories about Steve, I think it's fair to say there were some deeply rooted issues that he was wrestling with, some of which my Uncle Scott talked about at the beginning of the story. My father hid some of the more difficult emotions he was having after his sister passed, and he did the same in his battle with cancer. He pulled away emotionally and decided to shoulder the burden alone. I did not want this part of a book to read simply as a eulogy, a list of my father's attributes; I also wanted to share learnings we can take from his shortcomings. It appears this was an area where my father fell short.

Paul, John, and others saw Steve wrestling with his demons internally, but they could do nothing about it, as he did not go to them for help. He did not make himself vulnerable to those around him, even though there is no doubt that he was suffering. I have said it before, and I will say it again: do not follow in his footsteps. Sometimes, life is too overwhelming to carry the weight of your worries alone. That's what your loved ones are there for. No weight feels as heavy when it is shared with others. No matter the magnitude, no matter the drama, whether it's the loss of family or friends, or something more trivial, reach inside yourself and try to find a way to be open about it. Talk to a therapist or a friend – talk to anyone, for that matter. It helps.

Paul introduced Steve to his friend Gary, and years later, coincidentally, I became friends with Gary's son. Eventually, Steve,

Paul, and Gary formed a tight-knit friendship and even lived together before they all got married. They would hang out in their apartment with their girlfriends, as they began their adult lives together. And this is where my mother comes into the story.

Just as many of my father's friends, relatives, and colleagues have shared their perspectives on my father, it's only fitting to include the perspective of my mother's friends on Steve. I first spoke to my mother's best friend from college, Kathy Iannazo. Kathy and my mother first crossed paths while waiting in line for the keys to their freshman dorm room at Southern Connecticut State College in August 1982. The school later became a university before their graduation in 1986. Kathy and my mom became best friends and roommates during their sophomore year, a friendship that lasted well beyond college. They lived together in Norwalk during the first year after college when my mom worked as a Special Education teacher in Greenwich, Connecticut.

Kathy saw my father from a different perspective. She said he was always looking out for my mom's well-being, and that he had a kind of old-fashioned charm. She mentioned how Steve used to play the guitar for my mom. She used the word "woo." She said Steve wooed Lisa. Some people would interpret this as merely an act of flirtation, when in reality, it refers to an attempt to gain someone's trust in love, with marriage in sight. Let's stop and think about that for a moment. What it boils down to is trying to find your soulmate.

As the years rolled on, both Kathy and Lisa embarked on their journeys into married life and they and their partners started spending time together as couples. Steve played a pivotal role in assisting Kathy and her husband Steve in launching their local business, helping him to create their business plan. As life unfolded, they both started families – I was born; Kathy had her own kids – and although our families grew up side by side, our paths diverged: different lifestyles, diverse cultures, varied backgrounds. But no matter the differences, we had one commonality: we had trust in each other. These are the kinds of friends that are hard to come by in life. Then, my father died of cancer, and Kathy and Lisa's friendship grew stronger again, at least for a while. When we talked, she reminisced about her last memories of my father. She spoke of my father's funeral, and she, too, remembered the long line of people waiting outside the funeral home.

Her conclusion was simple. She said that my father was simply a remarkable man. He treated people with respect and was an all-around great guy.

As I relayed the conversations I had with many of my parents' friends and family, I think it's only right that we hear from my mother. Her perspective illustrates how she navigated her relationship with Steve, wearing both the hats of a wife and a friend.

Lisa Grove-Raider:

The way it affected me was simple: I needed to be the support network Steve needed. I could tell the illness weighed on him. I would try to keep busy and act normal to try to not let the stress affect him or Josh. As I started to watch him fade, I knew he was keeping certain feelings from everyone. By the very end, Steve was bottling up his emotions. If one of your loved ones is in a similar situation, then you can understand how this feels. I cannot stress the importance of speaking up and talking to other people. As I stated previously, you are not alone in your journey. Seek help, early and often. Be cognizant of the world around you and do not get lost in your own stress.

Josh Grove:

I spoke earlier about my first Relay for Life, back in 2002, during which my father spoke about beating cancer for the first time. Given that I was nine years old at the time, some of my memories of the event are a bit hazy. But the feeling I got as I watched my father speak in front of hundreds of people left an indelible impact on me. My mother and I recently sat and reminisced about the event, all these years later, and it brought us both incredible joy. She shared with me how special it was when we would go to these Relay for Life events together. In a way, for both of us, it was also a way to diverge the energy of stress into productivity, during Steve's various treatments. It helped us to stay optimistic. This was before the disease came back fiercer than ever.

Having to watch my father go through everything that he went through and then dealing with his passing took a toll on me. For a while, I felt lost. Then, throughout high school and college, I started to become more involved with various charities and organizations. My mother played an integral role in this. She was there helping to motivate me to push myself to achieve my goals, both big and small.

And becoming an active participant in the battle to end cancer had become one of my goals—perhaps the most important one. I knew there was a purpose behind why I was doing these events: to honor my father and lessen the suffering of people who are in the same position he had once been. Relay for Life became a huge part of both mine and my mother's lives. In this way, through his battle with cancer, Steve impacted our lives and continues to do so twenty years later, perhaps even more than he did when he was alive. I can remember one particular Relay for Life event at the University at Buffalo, where my close friends and I rallied around our team to raise the money to hit our goal. I remember how good it felt to help but also to inspire others.

As you read about Steve's final days, I want you to remember that the purpose of telling his story is to inspire you to go out there and try and make a difference. Helping to raise money for organizations that you are passionate about is a great way to do this – I strongly encourage you to look into your local charities! – but it doesn't have to be the only way. Identify what you really care about, find your *Why?*, and go take action.

Steve Grove:

Moving into the chemotherapy phase of my treatment was interesting. Everyone told me of the terrible side effects that will start the second they start loading you up on the drugs. Other than a little bloating and a runny nose, nothing happened. I suppose it's still early in the treatments. I have been relegated to two treatment phases of four weeks each, and two weeks' vacation for good behavior. They do 12 weeks and then retest to see if the nodules have disappeared and whether or not the cancer enzymes in your bloodstream have decreased. The combination of drugs I am on is very successful for what I have, and we are hopeful that my body will respond properly. There will be at least two treatment phases, if everything goes as planned, but we still don't know. There is always something to wonder about with this.

Josh Grove:

This was the point in my father's life where he was going through the toughest part of his battle with cancer. Even so, his close friends and family thought nothing was wrong. Steve never broke character: he would steer conversations away from him and focus on his friends and family. Whether he thought he knew his time was running out or not, he wanted the closest people in his life to not worry about him.

I was about seven or eight years old when my dad was first diagnosed. Throughout his struggle with cancer, no matter how bad he felt, he tried as hard as he could to be there for me, whether that was by showing up to watch my little league games or coming to watch me play at school. And he never stopped trying to be a mentor for me. Even in his final weeks, I can remember one time when I was being a bit "fresh" with my mom. He had moved back in because he couldn't take care of himself. He walked into my room and said, "Josh, please listen to your mother. Don't give her a hard time over something so little. Go and apologize to her." Even though he was struggling, he felt it was important to continue teaching me about what was important in life.

I strongly urge you to hold on to the people close to you and try to tell them something nice the next time you see them. Apologize when you're wrong, and most importantly, don't sweat the small stuff because life is too short. I want to pause here to share my mother's thoughts as she recalls Steve's final moments.

Lisa Grove-Raider:

I can remember the day vividly: where I was, where Josh was, and most importantly, where Steve was. I remember being in the hospital and how it felt. Steve fought to stay alive right up until the last second. At the very end, his organs were shutting down. The hospital staff tried to help him, but his lungs kept filling with fluid, and he struggled to breathe. He had previously signed a DNR, but in the end, he wanted to live: he asked his doctor to resuscitate his heart if it stopped. I will never forget the desperation in his eyes while he tried to remove the oxygen mask, right before he went into a deep sleep, never to wake up again. I remember holding his hand firmly and telling him, "It's okay. Josh, and I will be okay. You have had a tremendous impact on so many people's lives. You do not have to worry anymore. It's okay to let go now. We love you." That was one of the most emotional moments in my life and one of the hardest things I have ever gone through. The importance of living in the moment and cherishing the people who matter the most has never been so evident to me as it was in that moment.

It was difficult to look at Steve and not respect him; I am sure my son can attest to this as well. He was always trying to teach others. Even in his final moments, he was doing his best to support me and trying to help Josh grow and mature as a young man. To Steve's mind, that also included the serious side of life, and he would talk to Josh about the things that matter in life. Steve was always tremendously good at being able to compartmentalize his thoughts, emotions, and feelings. Whether that was a good or bad thing for him, I don't know, but it was something I respected about him: that he could put aside his worries in order to teach our son a valuable life lesson. It is something I did not cherish until years later.

If there is one thing I could say about both Steve and Josh, this would be it. The little things mattered the most to them. How their actions affected others mattered. How others felt mattered. They both knew that no matter how bad of a time you are having, it's important to notice and acknowledge other people's feelings, too. Remember, even if you're the only one standing, you are not the only one in the room; there are others, just sitting down.

Chapter 15: The Best Person You Can Be

Josh Grove:

When you look at your life from a bird's eye view, you will probably see your life's story differently than you had when you were living it. In your older years, you may look at your younger years, your teenage years, college experiences, young adulthood, and finally adulthood, and maybe not be able to relate to the person you used to be: each of us goes through many changes and many versions of ourselves in the great journey of life. But remember that every phase of your life has meaning and purpose, and each is important to your growth as a human being. My father's life was cut short at age 40. But I believe even though he did not get a chance to reach old age, his struggles and his own character forced him to reach inside himself and find true wisdom and grace, despite his relatively young age. He was a *mensch*.

When I was nine years old, my mom and I went to visit him in the hospital after his third treatment. I remember how excited he was to see us. More importantly, he wanted to show us that he was still fighting. He would ask me questions about school and homework. I will always remember what he told me:

"Josh, you don't have to worry about me. Soon, I'll be able to take you to baseball practice. I feel great and am going to be just fine!"

Although he never showed me he was afraid, I was still scared seeing him in the hospital with all those tubes and medical equipment. He didn't look the same. He had lost weight and had lost a lot of his hair. Nevertheless, he always tried to make it known that the person in front of him was always more important than he was. He would try to focus the conversation on you rather than discuss his health. My grandfather, Peter Patten, said to me years later, when I started writing this book: "Your father cared for everyone but himself."

This kind of selflessness and patience can have a profound impact on our lives and the lives of those around us. My father, a man of incredible character, exemplified these qualities in ways that continue to inspire me every day. But there is a bigger picture here that I want to stress.

Sometimes, when you look back on your life, you may find that there were moments in which your reactions were not what you wanted them to be, either because you were stressed, tired, hurt, or in pain, or maybe triggered by past trauma. Perhaps you were short with a friend or family member, or reacted with anger or defensiveness when someone tried to talk to you. You may think to yourself, "I wish I had acted more graciously in that situation" or, "I wish I had been more patient." I encourage you, as you read his story, to stop for a moment and ask yourself, "Are there any parallels here with hardships in my own life? Is there a way to see what I am going through from a different lens? Is it possible to react differently?" My goal of sharing with you his story was to pass along any learnings that I had from this experience—as well as from my father's experience with cancer. So I hope I have been able to push you to think about how you can apply these learnings to your own life. Remember, it is how you handle a situation that defines who you are. You cannot change a situation, rather, you must change how you react.

My father also had an appreciation for the little things in life, which he tried to pass on to me. We go through our days wrapped up in the day-to-day race, keeping our blinders up and focusing on the tasks at hand. On any given day, our time is filled with chores, work, and social activities. But rarely do we stop and appreciate those around us. Rarely do we stop and smell the flowers. In his commencement speech at Agnes Scott College in Decatur, Georgia, the writer Kurt Vonnegut tells an anecdote about his uncle Alex, who "did his best to acknowledge it when times were sweet. We could be drinking lemonade in the shade of an apple tree in the summertime, and Uncle Alex would interrupt the conversation to say, "If this isn't nice, what is?"[2] Vonnegut concludes his speech by encouraging his listeners to follow in his uncle's footsteps. "When things are going sweetly and peacefully, please pause a moment, and then say out loud, 'If this isn't nice, what is?'" I think my father would have liked this speech. I know he always stressed the importance of acknowledging and appreciating the good times. As he found out when he was diagnosed, you never know what comes next.

Now, can you take anything from this story? Take a moment to think about a situation where someone did something for you. You

---

[2] See: "If This Isn't Nice, What Is?: Advice to the Young" by Kurt Vonnegut

may or may not have thanked them at the time. Either way, looking back on it and knowing someone went out of their way to help you feels good, doesn't it? So why not say it? The next time someone goes out of their way for you, thank them. I promise you that it will go a long way. And why stop there? If someone helped you, pay it forward. Help someone else who is in need. You may even have someone who has been affected by cancer or another disease in your life and not know it. If you see that someone is feeling down, try to be there for them.

Cancer, of course, affects millions of people every day. And when someone is a sufferer, it is difficult to predict how they will handle the situation, how they feel, or what they may need. "Being there for them" can be as simple as spending quality time together, or as challenging as having to do something practical they need doing that may be out of your comfort zone. I can promise you one thing: your actions will go much further than you can imagine. Not only will this help the person in need, but it will help you, too. Again, as you hear about my father's last treatment and final days, try to think of the bigger picture, and apply the lessons you find herein to your own life and the journey towards growth.

Steve Grove:

People tell me that after you finish treatments, there is a feeling of disappointment and depression because you aren't doing anything. I suppose you will always wonder, with every six-months or yearly test, whether the cancer is back or whether any problems will show up again. They tell me that the further you go without any issues, the better off you are. I hope that this is true and that I can start moving forward.

My wife and I had planned to travel to Russia to adopt a baby boy and we hope that, if everything is clear after chemotherapy, we can find the strength to make this next journey. I often wonder if that is what life is all about, just moving from journey to journey.

Josh Grove:

My parents had tried several times to have another child and, after many disappointments, they started leaning towards adoption. They knew of a good adoption agency in Russia and as a young boy, I was hopeful to one day have a sibling of my own. After the excitement subsided, my mom suddenly told me they would no longer be going to Russia. "What? Why?!" I asked. She explained that my father simply did not have the strength to travel. My father was no longer sugarcoating how he felt at that point—unfortunately, the honesty came just as he was running out of time. He said to me: "Josh, I simply don't have the strength to go and am not doing as well as I'd hoped. Everything will be okay, though. Try and stay strong for your mother. *Always remember to never, ever give up."*

Steve passed away on June 20th, 2003. I was ten years old at the time. I will never forget that day: my mom woke me up by telling me my father was not feeling well and that she had called an ambulance. She said I should get up and call my friends because she had to go with him. I jumped out of bed and immediately ran to look outside the window. Sure enough, I saw two paramedics strolling up our lawn. I dressed and went into his room. He was sitting there with the paramedics and asked me to come over and hug him. He whispered into my ear: "Josh, I love you. Dad's gotta go. Be good for your mother. Stay strong for her, and remember, I will always be there for you." Then he said, "Never give up on yourself,' as he pointed directly at my heart. Even in his last moments with me, he was trying to pass on advice. I hugged him and said I loved him back, and then I left to spend the day with friends in the neighborhood.

Later that afternoon, I was playing video games at my friend Armand Sebastian's house. My mother contacted me on my Walkie Talkie – I was too young to have a flip phone and that was the only way our parents could reach us back in the day. She said, "Josh, please come home." Her voice was serious. I remember giving my friends a very confused look. Somewhere in the pit of my stomach, I almost knew something had happened, but I was unsure how to feel. I went home, walked through the door, and found my mom, my grandparents, my uncle, and a few family friends gathered in the living room. I remember wondering why everyone was there. My grandpa Peter and my mom sat me down on the couch and told me my father had passed away. He said that my dad wanted to tell me that he loved me and that he would always be with me. To this day, this was one of the toughest and most painful moments of my life. I urge you to be thankful for what you have; Try not to hold grudges and appreciate the little things in life. Even at that difficult moment in my life, having all my family and their friends around me made everything just a little bit easier.

On November 3rd, 2003, four and a half months after my father's death, I was called to receive a second posthumous award on his behalf. This was the James E. West Fellow Award from the Boy Scouts of America, a local award given to individuals who helped raise a certain amount of money for a specific charity. Receiving this award was both sad and weird for me, yet in retrospect happy at the same time. It was all still very confusing for me, but I saw on that day that my father was a well-appreciated man in the community. As I started to realize, on that day, the impact he had had on those around him and the effort he had put into giving back to the community that had supported him, I began to realize I also wanted to give back more. My father – though I would not realize this until years later – had laid the groundwork for me to grow into a better person. It's moments like these that, as an adult, I think about more and more. It is moments like these that have changed me. Accepting the award was not easy, but it is now a memory I hold dear to my heart.

Lisa Grove-Raider:

Watching Josh receive an award in Steve's name is something I will never forget. It was an emotional night, but one my son and I will cherish forever. I think it was one of those moments that had a bigger impact on me later in life. At the time, Steve's death was just so fresh that it was hard for all of us in that room that day to focus on the positive. Thinking back on it now, I am proud that people continued to cherish Steve Grove's memory and accomplishments after his passing. To this day, I think anyone associated with the Boy Scouts of America both domestically and internationally, remembers Steve Grove fondly.

When I first met Steve, he was Director of Camp Sequassen, and I was at Southern Connecticut State University finishing up my degree in special education. When I met him, I remember noting the immense pride he took in his work. He took his role as camp director seriously; often, he had to be the responsible one of the bunch. I can remember thinking that the staff and campers clearly respected him, but it was more than that. Everyone loved him at camp. He would play his guitar at meals in the dining hall or around the campfire. He would joke around with the others and try to make people laugh. Later, after he passed, I spent more time at Camp Sequassen with Josh. I acted as a chaperone, which was quite a different experience from that I had shared with Steve in my youth. But although Steve was not there with us, we both felt his presence. Getting to share this special place with my son – the place where Steve and I had met – is a gift that I will always cherish. It's a small thing, maybe, but isn't that what matters most? I think Steve would have agreed with this sentiment.

No misfortune, hassle, or struggle is the same; they are not measurable against one another. Sometimes, you may feel you have it worse than others and that no one can understand what you are going through. Dealing with a loved one affected by cancer can make you think like that, but I don't think that it's necessarily true. No matter what hardships you are facing, looking at how people around you deal with their own problems can give you important insights into how to deal with your own—even when the problems seem vastly dissimilar in nature or severity. To be able to do this, you have to be present. You have to be a part of the lives of those around you. You have to listen to them.

First, you need to try to find your inner peace and tap into whatever resources of patience you have at your command. You cannot help others if you are stressed and harried yourself; there is a reason they tell you to put your own oxygen mask on first in the event of an emergency on an airplane.

I tried to show my support to Steve, who I knew was struggling more than me, even if he did not show it. Whether by attending medical appointments, offering emotional or practical support, or simply spending more quality time with our family, I did my best to be there for him. This was only natural to me. But what impresses me most, looking back, is that Josh was doing this, too. Although he was only a child at the time, he was a rock for our family during this hard time. In a waiting room or similar places, he knew he had to be patient. When in the visiting hospital room, he knew he had to be calm so as not to exhaust his father. In short, he had learned from a young age what it means to put aside your own needs in order to help others. This was never more evident to me than while Steve was going through his treatments. Josh's patience and fortitude made things just that little bit easier.

So, even when life continues to throw you curveball after curveball, you can still rise up to the occasion and be your best self.

Josh Grove:

Cancer tests your limits. Finding your inner strength can be difficult. But knowing that by being strong you can help others to fight through pain can be a tremendous motivator. And your own pain can be helpful, in a strange way. There is a sort of strength that comes out of pain, strife, and struggle. You never know what emotional reserves you possess, what "stuff you're made of" until you are forced to test yourself. At some point, you reach a moment when you feel that there is nothing worse that can possibly happen. You can only go up from here, and so you continue to test yourself, to push your boundaries, to pull yourself through. I saw both my father and my mother being in those situations and rising admirably to the challenge of staying strong and positive, so I tried to emulate their examples. I strove to be the best person I could be, as I saw my parents trying to do. I urge you to take this bit of advice to heart in dark times. It doesn't not matter if you fail; the important thing is to try.

I chose to share Steve's story because of the impact I felt it could have and *has had* on my life. My father was what many people would call a *fixer*. There's a lot to unpack in that word. A fixer means someone who fixes things that are broken and repairs them to make them better, right? But it can also mean someone who enhances the potential of something or someone. It can also mean someone who builds something from the ground up. Many of the people I would hear from after Steve passed talked about being helped by him at one point or another. People would tell me how my father was there for them, gave them advice, or made them feel better about a particular situation. He helped some get started in their business or mentored them or their children. Steve left a tremendous legacy behind, but the thing that sticks out for me the most from all the stories I heard was his drive and ability to help people to *grow*. It's not just that he cared for those around him; it's that he also wanted them to be the best version of themselves. If he could get one friend to push himself to be one percent better, he was happy.

So, when hardship hits, do not let yourself become overwhelmed by stress and worry; reach inside yourself and strive for that one percent improvement. If you don't feel equal to the situation, think of how the best person you know would react if they were in your shoes, and then try to *be* that person. Remember the indomitable spirit of Jim Valvano's motto: "Never give up." As long as you feel you have done your best, you will truly feel better about yourself, your situation, and your life.

Chapter 16: Piecing It All Together

Josh Grove:

"You must have the enthusiasm for life. You have to have a dream, a goal. And you have to be willing to work for it." – Jim Valvano, ESPYS Speech on March 4, 1993.

That famous quote from Jim Valvano's speech has been up on a poster in my childhood room since I was in high school. I cannot stress enough how impactful that quote has been in my life. I know I have referenced *Jimmy V* quite often and for good reason. If you are reading this, I hope you can see the impact it has had in my life, and the relevance it could have in *your* life. I strongly suggest taking a minute to Google him and reading even one article about his legacy. This brings us to the final lesson and the final part of my father's life. I wanted to share how his legacy has helped me tie up all the loose ends, fill in all blanks, and let the story come full circle.

In August of 2016, thirteen years after my father died, my family and I were cleaning and packing our house in Rye Brook, New York, as we were getting ready to move to Stamford, Connecticut. My mother and I and a close friend of mine came across an unmarked box. The box looked rather dirty; I had never seen it before. Inside the box were seventy-five typed out pages that my father had written over the last few years of his life—the unfinished manuscript for the book he had intended to publish. My mother, it turns out, already knew about this book, and so did a handful of people who had been very close to my father. For me, it was like finding lost treasure.

No digital copy of this existed; perhaps this added to the feeling of unearthing something precious. It would have been maybe different if I'd found this on an old computer. As it was, I flipped through the journal in amazement. I would get to read my father's story, through his own eyes! I could hear his "voice," his thoughts, his speech patterns, after all these years! I sat down and started to read the first few pages and knew immediately that this had the markings of something special. I thought, if I could share this with other people who were struggling, maybe his writing could help them get through some of the darkest times of their lives. The idea occurred to me that it could be a collaborative effort between my father and me—that I could help fill in the gaps missing from the story. I realized it would not be possible for me to do this alone; after all, when he passed, I was only ten years old. Therefore, to get the full picture I had to bring in people who truly knew Steve. They would help paint a fuller picture and cover different periods of his life that I could not provide a perspective on.

I knew it would not be an easy task. This was uncharted territory for me. I didn't know how I would go about finding those who had known him. On top of that, I had never written a book and had no idea where to start. Little did I know that writing this book truly was an opportunity to get the closure I didn't even know I really needed. The people I met or re-met for the purposes of this project brought me new and refreshing opinions on my father, and not only helped with the book but were also instrumental in my personal growth. Some of his closest friends were able to connect the dots or clarify things I had always wondered about, or shared stories about him that were similar to my recollections of him and helped solidify some of my memories. And me interacting with my father, albeit through our writings, after all this time, helped me to process certain feelings and thoughts I had only been unconsciously aware of up to that point. Most importantly, some of the stories I heard showed me how similar I am to my father.

Steve Grove:

The warning booklets that they give you warn you of many side effects and issues that could come up. The guys at work say they can't imagine me bald. But I wonder what I will look like... if that happens. I try to stay positive and urge you to do so as well. Throughout your ordeal, seek within yourself that strength that you never thought you had. You would be amazed at what the human spirit can endure.

Josh Grove:

When I started to put together this story, I decided that was going to be one of my goals: to show how I connected my father's values to my life and personal growth. One thing that became clear from these writings was that my father was always thinking ahead, even when there was no reason to be optimistic. That is a mentality

I've fully embraced. The notion of constantly considering what's next and planning for the future was a valuable lesson he instilled in me. Developing the skill to mentally juggle tasks will provide the competitive edge you need and help you achieve your goals. Personally, I've made it a goal to hone this ability. I urge you to do the same. Embrace what's right in front of you, but also keep an eye on the next task at hand. Whether it's a work project, a personal fitness goal, or brightening someone's day, they all hold significance and purpose. Achieving these smaller goals will pave the way for more substantial victories. Remember, don't get caught up in the minor details. Progress will come with its fair share of failures and obstacles. The key is to never give up on yourself. Life has its ups and downs. It's your responsibility to pause along the way and find an appreciation for the little things, particularly acknowledging how each experience contributes to your personal growth. Muster the mental fortitude to persevere, as it will ultimately make you a stronger person.

Let me make myself clear: when I talk about being forward-thinking, I'm not suggesting that living in the moment should be avoided. Life is a journey, and a short one at that, and we are all just here for the ride. So why not try to live life to the fullest? Savor every moment, especially moments spent with the people you love, and don't dwell on *might-have-been*s. You don't want to miss what's standing right in front of you. So if you take one lesson from this, let this be it: never dwell on the past; relish the present; but never stop dreaming about what lies ahead.

Another thing I learned from my father was the importance of laughter. Steve always endeavored to infuse humor into his life, both when I was little and during his battle with cancer. Anyone acquainted with Steve can attest to his distinct dry sense of humor and his lightheartedness among friends. This made it exceptionally easy for me to connect with his sense of humor. I have a story here I would like to relate:

When I was young, I wanted to know why I grew up a Yankee fan—my maternal grandfather and most of my relatives on my mother's side supported the Red Sox, while my father's side of the family had always supported the Yankees. So, my grandfather told me this story: many moons ago, he was on his sailboat off the coast of Martha's Vineyard with my grandmother, when he got a call from my father telling them their grandchild was about to be born. My mom wanted them to come home to the hospital, so he and my grandmother turned their boat around. They arrived at Yale New Haven Hospital in New Haven the following day. My grandfather walked into the hospital room with a Red Sox yearbook in his hand, which he placed on the bed. It was his first present to me. My father gave him a curious look. "What is this?" he asked. He picked it up and tossed it out of the door and into the hallway saying, "No son of mine will grow up a Red Sox fan!" Then he pulled out a Yankee hat and put it right on the bed next to my mother and me.

For many people, that story may bring a light chuckle or maybe a smirk, but to my father, it was the funniest thing in the entire world. He had just told his father-in-law off and showed him who was the boss. That was just who he was. My grandpa told me that story with such joy; he had always appreciated my father's sense of humor. He told me that my father grew up as a die-hard Yankee fan and that he would have wanted the same for me. From the moment I heard that story, I knew that for the rest of my life my team would be the New York Yankees.

Before I try to wrap up this chapter, I wanted to let other people take the floor. From them, you will hear stories that range through various timeframes of my father's life. Some of the people I spoke to told me they had been greatly affected by his passing and were happy to get the opportunity to reminisce about Steve. They were eager to share their stories with me when I contacted them some 16–18 years afterward. Many of these stories will be of his major accomplishments, some as he neared the end of his life, and some after he passed.

Paul Ryder's perspective on Steve Grove

Steve was a great friend and a peer mentor to me. We met through scouting in our teens. Then our friendship grew from there through life's journey of high school, college, careers, marriages, and kids. We went on trips together, camped together, had double/triple dates together, and were in each other's wedding parties – all the things great friends do. Steve was driven and smart. He had a big heart and a positive attitude, and he was always fun to be with. Thank you, Josh, for pulling these fond memories back to the forefront for me.

Chuck Sullivan's perspective on Steve Grove

Thinking about Steve Grove has often brought me to tears—and not just out of sadness, but also because of the joy he brought into my life. Steve was a guidepost for me. He possessed many great qualities, but if I had to pinpoint what he was best at, I'd say it was networking. It was a characteristic Steve Grove truly embodied. He just knew exactly how to connect with people, build rapport, and make others feel comfortable around him. Steve had a tremendous impact on my life, which continues even now. I wish he were here today so that I could thank him for being him.

David Gordon's perspective on Steve Grove

Steve was one of my closest friends. His loyalty, love of life, and his ability to care deeply about others are what made him so special. He had an intensity about him that could be overwhelming. He had no tolerance for those who crossed him or crossed the people he loved. Mostly though, I smile at remembering all the times he would "go for the joke" or see the humor and silliness in day-to-day life. This, more than anything, was the bond that connected us. I often think about all the times since his death when we would have cracked each other up. Although I miss Steve immensely, I'm grateful that I get to share those times now with his son, Josh.

X's perspective on Steve Grove [X has chosen to remain anonymous]

Steve Grove was simply unforgettable to me and all who knew him at Congregation Or Shalom. I first met Steve when he was interviewed by our Youth Committee for the position of Kadima Youth Advisor. And even then, it was obvious that we were interviewing a young man (he was around twenty years old at the time) who was an idealist: Steve told us he wanted to make an impact on the next generation and keep them within Judaism. He wanted to let Jewish teenagers know that "Judaism *cared* about them." It was quite

186

clear even then that he was not just looking for a job or some "college gig," but responding to a calling he felt within himself. In fact, I remember that some on the Youth Committee were a bit intimidated by Steve's intensity: At one point in the interview, he chided us for not responding sooner to his application! "I wrote to you and followed up with a call; and now, we've lost some time," he lamented! The intensity he evidenced in that interview never diminished through the years he served as our Youth Advisor. And looking back and speaking for the teenagers who were lucky enough to have had him as their leader, Steve succeeded in his mission: He conveyed his message quite clearly to them: "*Judaism truly cares about you.*"

Adam Kligfeld's perspective on Steve Grove

Steve Grove was one of the first adults in my life who paid attention to me as a teenager. He showed me he cared and had a true interest in who I was. He did not hold back praise and encouragement, but nor was he afraid to let me know when I had done the wrong thing. This pushed me to aspire to be better. He was both a friend and mentor and clearly a role model. He opened his home and his heart to me and many others. He helped push me towards being the responsible, caring, devoted, and Jewish-ly proud teenager I turned out to be.

I am not sure what I enjoyed more: laughing with him or making him laugh. He had humor in his own right, and he could crack me up with one-liners or witticisms. But he was also a tremendous audience for my humor. It was enormously satisfying to have him break into a full-body chuckle when I landed a good line. Steve was great and also humble. He knew he was not a Jewish scholar, per se. Yet he pushed me and my peers towards greater and deeper Jewish connection and learning. He was tremendously proud of me when I achieved and did something worthy. He kicked my behind and lovingly chided me for it when we played racquetball. He gave me lessons on leadership, independence, and maturity, weaving his Boy Scouts identity with his Jewish youth leader role. He believed in me, and that helped me believe in myself.

His loss remains a great pain in my life. His continued presence in my life remains an even greater blessing.

Ellen and Ed Beatty's perspective on Steve Grove

Ellen's Perspective: My relationship with Steve was a unique one. Our friendship was a journey of energy, love, and laughter, yet always looking forward. We were great friends together. We spent time at camp together, shows, dinners, and many other events. We were part of each other's lives. We both knew each other's hidden strengths, which made our friendship that much stronger. Steve really knew how to make the best of a situation, which I truly admired.

Ed's perspective: I always felt positive about Steve when I was around him. We had a lot of great success collaborating with some of the scouting events. I liked being around Steve. He was such a delight to be around.

Linda Spivack's perspective on Steve Grove

Steve Grove taught me about humanity and selflessness. He was a man who had a lot of integrity. One evening when Steve, Lisa, my husband George, and I were out for dinner at a local place in the New Haven area in Connecticut, Steve said something to the waiter. What he had said was, "No, I can't have that dish because of the pine nuts." Steve then shared that they had seen something on a test he had, "a shadow,

hopefully just diverticulitis." That was the first time I saw fear, concern, sadness, and hope on Steve's face all at once. If you knew Steve, you knew that his dark thick mustache and curly hair couldn't hide his feelings.

That was the beginning of a different kind of friendship between us. Steve knew I was a "cancer nurse," and I will always treasure what he taught me. Steve tried every way to stay well, and he searched for any option and cure. He faced his adversity with courage and focused on everyone else, especially on Josh. We all have secrets, ones that we never expect to have to share. Yet as Steve faced his own horror, he taught us all how to love, and he taught me personally how to not judge, how to be true to myself, and how to work for what I believe in. He also taught me how to ask for forgiveness, how to fight injustice in the world, and how to give to others no matter what.

May Steve's memory be a blessing and source of strength for the work we all must do in order to make this world a more just, caring, loving, and peaceful place—as Steve strived to do every day of his short life. Josh Grove will carry on Steve's legacy; may God grant him a life filled with health and happiness.

Josh Grove:

Everyone who shared their experiences and stories about my father has also had a lasting effect on me. These are the people that I have personally shared funny moments, sad moments, and moments of reflection with—moments which have shaped me into the person I am today.

My last and final story for you will bring closure to our story. Moreover, it will be the last piece of advice I share with you. I have talked a lot about me and my father's passion for sports, our shared love for the Yankees and our admiration for Jim Valvano. I want to return one last time to Jimmy V, and share a final quote that may shed light on the overall message of this book. When receiving his ESPYs Arthur Ashe Courage Award for his battle with cancer, Jimmy V said:

*"If you **laugh**, you **think**, and if you **cry**, that's a full day. That's a heck of a day. You do that seven days a week, you're going to have something special...."*[3]

People who've known me a long time know that I always try to not take things too seriously. Like my father, I try to look on the bright side of life, and take great joy and comfort in humor; at the end of the day, laughing is one of the healthiest things you can do for yourself. When I read that quote for the first time, I thought, "Laughter, tears, and self-reflection. Wow. Jim Valvano gets it." Let's take those one thing at a time. If you laugh about something, it usually means you are experiencing happiness. If you cry (whether you're happy or sad) just for a second, it means you're vulnerable. When you're vulnerable you're raw and can deal with your emotions. Lastly, when you spend time in thought on a given day, it means you're trying to make yourself or a situation better. You are growing. Being able to do all

---

[3] ("Jim's 1993 ESPY Speech", YouTube, V Foundation).

three will help you get through any situation. But being able to laugh at yourself and maintain positivity is the one that is hardest when you are suffering and in pain. My father knew it was important, though. See, humor and laughter is not about avoiding tough emotions or never feeling down. It is about embracing the full emotional roller coaster that is life. If you can do that, your capacity to grow will be limitless. Much like being forward-thinking and living in the moment, embracing both life's pain and life's humor are not mutually exclusive things. They go together: both are crucial to the human experience, and both are ingredients of a life lived to its fullest.

So, in summary, here's your life. Live it. Feel your sadness when it's warranted, but try not to sweat the small stuff. Enjoy and appreciate those around you. And try to laugh, cry, and think once a day—that, to my mind, is a life well-lived.

Epilogue

Josh Grove:

Throughout the years, our world has been faced with many challenging obstacles: the attacks of 9/11, Poliovirus, COVID-19, World Wars, the list goes on. What is the commonality amongst these tragic life events? How we remember. How we move on. How we rebuild. How we adapt. How we survive.

Struggle always turns our lives upside down. My father's vision for his life and future was never realized; one does not plan to get cancer. One does not plan to be inside a burning building. One does not plan to get sick with a deathly disease. Disaster is always unexpected. But we roll with the punches. We rebuild, adapt, and survive.

Now, whether you are currently going through a difficult time or not is irrelevant; suffering is one of life's few certainties. Tough times hit everyone, no matter the shape your suffering may take. When they come, try to turn your pain and negativity into constructive motivation. As soon as you start to take action, you will find yourself in a better mental place than you did when you started. Remember that this story is about more than just one man's battle with cancer. I have shared that I believe my father and I were alike. Although the way we dealt with difficult situations was different, the underlying themes and lessons you can walk away from our personal struggles are similar.

Everyone has their own individual coping mechanisms and their own way of dealing with problems. As long as you stay true to yourself and act according to your *why*, you will find the answers you are looking for. Look to your loved ones for advice, companionship, and comfort, but remember that you are your own best asset. Learn to trust yourself. And when you feel that the struggle you are going through has opened up a chasm between your life now and the future plans you had made, fill that void with calculation. Convince yourself that you are okay, then step back, take a deep breath, and make a plan. Life will keep throwing you curveballs and confuse the heck out of you. But remember that, as cliché as it sounds, whatever doesn't kill you makes you stronger. So don't ever, ever give up.

Acknowledgments

There's an old saying that I like to live my life by: never change your goal, change your plan. In my life, I have always been very goal-oriented, and the writing of this book was treated no differently. Having an opportunity to live out my father's legacy through this book has been truly both cathartic and remarkable at the same time, and a journey I never thought I would get a chance to embark on. I will always be grateful to this group of people for guiding me through and seeing me safe on the other side.

First, I want to thank Andy Chasanoff, for truly sharing this process with me truly from start to finish. I think back to that infamous night when the idea for this book first came to me, many years ago, when we first uncovered my father's writings. We both had no idea what would come of this. I never thought that the rough idea we talked about would come to life. It was truly a dream to get this opportunity to do this. For that, I want to thank him for always being there to support me and motivate me to finish this journey.

Max Holm and Melissa Coluccio are two people whose encouraging words had a tremendous impact on me over the years. The two of them always found a way to constantly look for updates and push me to the finish line. Max and Melissa, your subtle encouragement helped me keep that fire going. For that, I am forever grateful to you both. It also never hurt that two of my best friends decided to get married. So, your words of wisdom would come in twos, and therefore it was even more valuable!

Alec Bogholtz and Evan Glickman have been a part of this process in unique ways. Alec was there that infamous day in Washington Square Park when I first put pen to paper. I owe these two a major thank you for putting up with me, as I would write tirelessly, be on the phone constantly, and always want to converse about my new findings. There's such a sense of happiness when the people you live with are always there for you and keep pushing you to do better, so thank you for that.

Dan Fishman is a friend who provided some very pivotal parts in the book. His unique ability to always get through to me always resonated. I appreciate your encouragement over the years, your help in talking through crucial ideas, and your constant willingness to help when I wanted to talk about my thoughts.

Jacob Smart, Eric Mauro, Brandon Werner, and Brendan Morse, I owe you a major thank you for your friendship. The four of you would always ask about my progress and where I was on my journey—never pushing or prying, but always providing the needed support no matter where I was. Thank you for your unconditional support.

There is one individual that I want to take a moment to thank especially, and that person is John Petrillo. As 2020 began, I had an idea of reaching out to hundreds of my father's close friends. However, I was not sure where to start. He was the first person I spoke with about this journey, the first to come up with an idea for how to go about this, and he wanted to do everything in his power to help. He helped me reach out on social media. Without a match to light the fire that was my initial idea, we may not have had as many stories in this novel. His contribution was vital to both my personal growth and the growth of this book. I want you to know the impact you had on me on that very COVID-ridden day. I hope you know how appreciative I am of you. You were the first and, in many ways, the most influential domino here, and for that I thank you.

My mother, Lisa Grove-Raider, and my stepfather Peter Raider are two people I owe a great deal to. They were not only the best parents a kid could ask for but also incredibly supportive of me during the writing of this book. This process was not easy: there were many hours of thoughts, conversations, extensive research, and a lot of soul-searching. But each step along the way, you were both there pushing me, picking me up when I was down, and just being top-notch cheerleaders. For that, I am forever in debt to you both and love you very much. Thank you to my mother for your countless hours of editing and reviewing to help bring this story to life. Without your invaluable help in just about everything, I could not have done this.

Steve's brother and my uncle, Scott Grove, played an important part in this journey. When I first started putting pen to paper, I knew deep down that he would have a unique story to tell, given that this book was written about my father posthumously. He was the only one who was there from the day my father was born (they were almost nine years apart) until the final day of my father's life. Scott provided a grounding perspective for our audience, and I cannot thank him enough for the time he put into this book. His vantage point was one that no one else could have shared with me. Throughout the years working on this book, there were various instances where Scott and I would discuss my father. He told me one story about the fact that he and my father never played golf together. That story stuck with me, because it was something new, something I didn't know about my father. When my uncle agreed to add a small piece to this book, I was thrilled. I knew it would and could add to the complexity of the story and make the book better as a whole. We both knew that his angle would be different but necessary in order to tell my father's story with honesty and courage. I genuinely could not have finished this project, journey, and story without him. For this, I am forever grateful to my uncle for continuing to play such an important part of my life over the years. Scott, you have always been a father figure for me and a great mentor. We may not have always been living in the same state, but we have always stayed close, and that is why I am most grateful for our relationship. Your input really brought out the true meaning of this story, particularly as it relates to finding your purpose and your *Why?* in life. I could not have done this without you.

The final person I would like to thank is Emily Seitz—my other half, my partner in crime, my number #1 cheerleader, my everything. I cannot thank you enough for your unwavering support over the years. Your attitude, motivation, and comments have always kept me driven to finish this journey. I know I was probably not the easiest to deal with during this process, given how committed I was to finishing this story, but you mirrored that commitment every step of the way. Having you by my side the entire time gave me a sense of comfort and fueled my excitement about the book, knowing you were sharing every bit of this process with me. The best coincidence of it all is that the weekend I started putting ideas down on paper and began this book was the first week we started dating. I can remember telling you that I was going to Washington Square Park to write. Little did either of us know what would come next. I also owe you a major thank you for helping me grasp the concept of "perception is reality," which turned out to play a major role in this story. I love you and appreciate you for everything.

As you can imagine, there were many other people who helped along the way, important role models, mentors, and family members who helped piece the pieces of this story together. The first group to thank is the entire Grove & Patten families. Without any of you, this story would have never been written, and I appreciate every one of you. I have had many mentors along the way who have helped with anything from perspective to marketing ideas, and I appreciate all of you as well. To the many friends, colleagues, work friends, Sequassen friends, United Synagogue friends, and the many other youth-group friends of my father's, never forget that this story could not have been written without you. I spent many, many hours over the phone talking to all of you. So, David Gordon, John Petrillo, Marc Patten, Paul and Kim Ryder, Rabbi Adam Kligfeld, Caryl Kligfeld, Chris Nowacki, Jon Stengel, Ellen and Ed Beatty, Linda Spivack, Eric Green, Dena Shulman-Green, Paul Kallmeyer, Paul Boggush, Betsy Gorman, John and Josephine Farley, Chuck Sullivan, Charlie and Vivian Sullivan, Kathy Ianazzo, Rabbi Benjamin Scolnic, Rabbi X, Marty Ruest, Dan Groth, Billy Vincent, Steve Fahy, Bill Cramer, Ray Bendici, David Smith, and Jonathan Glassman, among many others, thank you. I also want to give a special shoutout and thank you to Dylan Breger for helping with the production and marketing efforts of this book. Thank you also to Amy Duncan, the creative designer of the book, and Eliza Ariadne Kalfa, who edited the book from start to finish. All of you have had such an impact on my personal life and this book. I cannot thank you enough for your help. As I wrap this up, I just want to say, to the many others who played a role in Steve's life, as well as my own: your work and thoughts were not forgotten and did not go unnoticed.

Works Cited

1. Chen, Helen. "Advances in Colorectal Cancer." *WebMD*, WebMD, 2004

2. January 12, 2022, et al. "Colorectal Cancer Rising among Young Adults." *National Cancer Institute*, 5 Nov. 2020

3. Martin, Laura J. "Breast Cancer Assessment: Dealing with Breast Cancer?" *WebMD*, WebMD, 12 Nov. 2017

4. Siegel, Rebecca L., et al. "Colorectal Cancer Statistics, 2020 - Wiley Online Library." *CA: A Cancer Journal for Clinicians CA: A Cancer Journal for Clinicians*, 5 Mar. 2020.

5. Robinson, Jennifer. "Stage IV Colon Cancer Prognosis." *WebMD*, WebMD, 27 Jan. 2020

6. TheVFoundation. "Jim's 1993 Espy Speech." YouTube, YouTube, 28 Sept. 2008

7. ESPN. "Jim Valvano's Espy Speech (1993) | 2020 Jimmy V Week for Cancer Research." *YouTube*, YouTube, 9 Dec. 2020

8. Dalio, Ray. Principles: Life and Work. Simon and Schuster, 2017

Made in the USA
Columbia, SC
16 December 2023

28709354R00119